Gafney imaginatively fills in
illuminating the meaning of stories written centuries ago. Jesus struggles to live up to his father's reputation as gifted carpenter; Peter and Paul debate dietary restrictions; Mary Magdalene feels fearful about visiting the tomb. Stories are followed by reflections, sample prayers and questions for group discussion. An essential companion for readers who wish to enhance and deepen the Christian spiritual journey.

Helen Klein Ross, *best-selling author of* ***What Was Mine*** *and* ***The Latecomers***

Scripture, stories, imagination, reflections, inspiration, and challenge—all this and more can be found in *I Am with You Always*! There might be a tendency to say, "I don't need another book on living my faith." How inaccurate that is. One of the greatest gifts embedded in these pages are the captivating, imaginative stories of what might have happened behind the scenes of many Scripture passages. These visionary tales connect Scripture and faith, then and now, and spirituality and our everyday life. Be prepared for new insights, challenging questions, and renewed fidelity.

Janet Schaeffler, OP, *retreat and adult formation presenter; author of several books, including* ***Let This Be the Time*** *and* ***The Catechist's Guide to Beloved Catholic Prayers***

Gafney reflects here on treasured remarks of Jesus recorded in the New Testament, each of them spoken face-to-face to individuals or groups in the orbit of his influence. These words are gifts from Jesus to the early Church. Gafney's reflections help us hear their power to nourish both the faithful and the seeker. Anyone praying with these texts will hear other words with fresh ears, words in their own hearts, and inspiring words, too, spoken to them by others.

George Bur, SJ, *senior member of the St. Joseph's University Campus Ministry Team*

I Am with You Always will be an excellent resource for individuals and Scripture-based faith sharing groups. In Part I, through expanded parables, readers are invited to enter into Jesus' first-century world, enabling a better understanding of Jesus' words. In Part II, through the use of twenty-first-century images, readers are encouraged to relate the Scriptures to our current world. Together, these parts will lead to fruitful mediation and faith sharing.

Gary and Beth Schwarzmueller,
Scripture-based faith sharing leaders, Westerville, OH

If you're looking to explore the historic truths of the gospel in ways relevant to contemporary life, consider Leo Gafney's creative new devotional book *I Am with You Always*. It offers two approaches, one presenting imaginative first-person narrations of the situations behind familiar biblical texts, the other explaining hard-to-grasp theological concepts by using varied and rich illustrations, ranging from the life cycle of monarch butterflies, to evolution and scientific knowledge. This engaging book, useful for personal or group study, will deepen your love of Scripture and enhance your life of prayer.

Dr. Rich Reifsnyder,
book author and Presbyterian minister

I Am with You Always

Stories of Jesus to Inspire Deeper Prayer

Leo Gafney

Twenty-Third Publications
One Montauk Avenue, Suite 200
New London, CT 06320
(860) 437-3012 or (800) 321-0411
www.twentythirdpublications.com

Copyright ©2021 Leo Gafney. All rights reserved.
No part of this publication may be reproduced in any manner without prior written permission of the publisher.
Write to the Permissions Editor.

The Scripture passages contained herein are from the *New Revised Standard Version Bible,* Catholic edition.
Copyright ©1989, by the Division of Christian Education of the National Council of the Churches of Christ in the U.S.A.
All rights reserved.

ISBN: 978-1-62785-644-7
Printed in the U.S.A.

CONTENTS

PART I
Jesus and His Times

PART II

Images and Parables for Our Time

INTRODUCTION

This book has several interconnected goals. The first is to awaken in the Christian reader curiosity and interest in Sacred Scripture. It is unfortunately true that we as Catholics have generally not been committed Bible readers. Some of us shrug, "The Bible is for evangelicals, fundamentalists." No, we should not think that way. The Bible, Sacred Scripture, is the word of God, given to instruct, encourage, and strengthen us in our faith as individuals and in community. Even more important, Scripture helps us pray; it gives us the words, stories, and situations that reveal God's work in this world—the world we share with God.

But perhaps like many Catholics you have found it difficult to read Scripture. Either you have heard the stories a hundred times and they still don't resonate with you, or if you are working at it, the language and situations are just strange enough to be off-putting. And so you can't "get into it."

I am very glad that you have this book in your hands. Let me tell you how it is different from other books and, more important, how it can help you to appreciate Scripture and to grow in faith. In the first section of the book, each chapter includes an incident, a short story perhaps, that is not historical. It is an exercise of the Christian imagination, something I invented. But each of these fictional accounts is directly connected to a situation in the New Testament, generally an incident from the life of Christ. The stories lead into or grow out of the Scripture text. These stories are intended as aids to lead you the reader to wonder what was happening in the past and so to explore your faith in the present. I hope these exercises will lead to a greater love of the gospels and to a richer life of meditation and prayer. The situations are accompanied by readings from the gospels or other New Testament writings, as well as the reflections of Christians through the ages.

Everyone loves a story. Jesus knew this and so he crafted remarkable narratives—brief, to the point, and powerful. The good Samaritan comes upon an injured man and tends to him. The prodigal son goes off and squanders his inheritance. These stories hold our minds and hearts. They tell us something about what God is like and how we can come closer to God in Christ.

Creating stories about Jesus is not new. St. Ignatius Loyola suggests that when meditating on a gospel passage we use a "composition of place" to fasten our attention. We picture the scene, the people, the countryside, or the buildings; we imagine what the people are saying and how they respond to one another. He and many others over the centuries have imagined what might have been, even placing themselves in the situation.

In this book the imagined incidents are inspired by and build on gospel stories. They are not meant to stand on their own or simply to stir the imagination. The brief fictional accounts are meant to throw light on gospel encounters that are often very brief, leaving us wanting more. What kinds of people were these? Why did they do the things they did? How might they speak to us?

A few words are needed about centurions. Israel in Jesus' time was an occupied country. Judea, the southern province was ruled directly by a Roman governor. Galilee, in the north, where Jesus grew up, is sometimes called a client state, ruled by Herod Antipas with the help of mercenaries or auxiliaries—volunteers, a common arrangement across the empire. Galilee was, of course, also answerable to Rome. Some commentators opine that the "centurion" described in the gospels was likely such a mercenary. The centurions are in fact generally described in the New Testament in favorable terms. The one in the gospel incident we refer to is said to have been favorably disposed toward Israel and to have built a synagogue for the people. The question of whether centurions might have had wives while serving is much debated. There seems to be enough evidence, particularly in the mercenary situation to support the possibility of the story as invented and presented here.

After the fictional incidents and New Testament readings, we reflect on the situations, sometimes with comments of Christians who have reflected on the Scriptures. For example the *Letter to Diognetus,* written in the second century, gives advice still relevant, connecting us to centuries past and to the teachings of Jesus.

> Happiness does not consist in ruling over one's neighbors or in longing to have more than one's weaker fellowmen. Nor does it consist in being rich and in oppressing those lowlier than oneself. No one can imitate God by doing such things. They are alien to his sublimity.

In the second part of the book we use our Christian imagination in a different way. We explore images and symbols. What might "light from light" mean? We can think of it as referring to the sun. What might be three dimensions that could help us think about and pray about the Father, Son, and Spirit?

We also look for new images and symbols that might help us understand the unseen world of the Spirit. We explore articles of faith and situations in Christian living based on our knowledge of the world around us. We do not expect to create images that are better than the ones Jesus left us. But as Christians we are compelled to continue seeking the meaning of his life and teachings in our midst and for our time. Each generation must reawaken the great insights and understandings of faith.

Each chapter contains questions. They can be used for group discussion or for you as an individual to consider what has been presented and how it might fit into your life. There is also a prayer at the end of each chapter that can be used by you as an individual or in a group context.

PART I

Jesus and His Times

1

A Carpenter

BUILDING A SPIRITUAL LIFE

WE KNOW ALMOST NOTHING ABOUT WHAT HAS BEEN CALLED THE HIDDEN LIFE OF JESUS. Like Joseph, he was a carpenter until he was about thirty years old, when he began his public life with his baptism by John. We know from his stories, sayings, and parables that Jesus was an astute observer of the world around him—the world of nature, work, and personal relationships. He commented on the flowers, children at play, men involved in their businesses, and women at home. The following is based on our understanding of Jesus' personality and how he often responded to people. It takes place when he is in his late twenties. With the leadership qualities we see in the gospels, it is not hard to imagine Jesus as the leader of his work crew. Carpenters of the time were also builders.

Jesus and his coworkers had spent a long day rebuilding a neighbor's barn that had been worn down by the years and the weather. It was hard work, and as Jesus bid his workers a pleasant evening, he remembered that he had one more thing to do before going home. He walked across the village, then out of town for about ten minutes, to the home of Samuel, whom he knew but not very well. Jesus' cousin had told him that Samuel was not happy with a new door they had made and installed.

Jesus arrived at Samuel's property and found him collecting rocks—perhaps to clear the land or to expand his hearth. Samuel was not young, but he remained strong and vigorous.

Jesus spoke, "Good evening, Samuel, I trust you and your family are well?"

"Deborah and the girls are well, thank you, and your mother? She is, well, still missing Joseph, I think?"

"Yes, it has been nearly two years now, but we do miss him very much—at home and, of course, at work."

Samuel continued the thought, "He was a gifted carpenter. I mean you are good, hard working and all. But he . . . ." His voice trailed off.

"It's true," said Jesus, "He made building seem effortless. He had a vision too. Whether it was a house, a barn, furniture, even toys. He could see what would work best and then know exactly how to do it. I was lucky to learn from him. It hasn't come as easily to me. As you say, he had a gift. The more I work, the more I appreciate him. In fact, I am still learning from what he taught me years ago. But what is the problem?"

"The problem," Samuel said, "is that the new door doesn't fit right. It scrapes on the bottom and leaves space at the top. It's crooked."

Jesus' crew had built a new door to replace the one that was worn and had recently been smashed in by soldiers making their rounds and inspecting. The old door had also stuck, Jesus remembered. Several of Jesus' crew had installed the door, and Jesus had not looked at it since.

"Let's have a look," Jesus commented as they walked toward the house. The door did indeed appear to be crooked. It stuck.

"Well?' Samuel asked.

"Well, I think we should do some measuring. And they did. Much to Samuel's surprise, the three measurements of the width—top, bottom, and middle were exactly the same. And measurements also showed that the height was not crooked or warped.

"One more." Jesus said. He measured the diagonal from top left to bottom right. This turned out to be the same as the other diagonal.

"There is nothing wrong with the door," Jesus said. "Let's measure the doorway."

"You think the doorway is crooked? You think my whole house is crooked? Jesus, do you know who built this house?'

"I believe it was my father: I helped. It was a long time ago." Jesus answered.

"Indeed, it was," chimed in Samuel, "Some years ago, and as we have said, he was an outstanding carpenter and builder."

Jesus listened but he also began measuring. The three measurements of the width of the doorway were the same, as were the three measurements of the height. But the diagonals were not. They were different by about the width of thumb.

"How can this be?" asked Samuel. "Joseph did not build crooked houses."

"Was this plot for the house given to you by your father?" asked Jesus, seeming to change the subject. "And were your choices of where to place the house rather limited?"

"Indeed, that was the case, and so?"

"I think my father did as well as he could—or as well as anyone could have done. But this is loose and sandy soil. He sank posts and used rocks as well as he could for a foundation but over time the sandy base has shifted a little bit. It's always better to build on rock—when we can. We will build a new doorway, but we also need to reinforce the house. You recall what happened to Shimon's house a few years ago. It was built on sandy soil."

"Well do I remember the collapse of Shimon's house. It was a disaster. Yes, I do remember Joseph commenting on the spot where he had to build. But let me ask, will I be expected to pay for this fixing and new doorway?" There was the slightest edge in Samuel's voice.

"I don't think so," said Jesus with an easy smile. "Suppose I come over with a few men after work for the next week or so, in the evening. Deborah might want to fix a light supper for the crew. And we will make straight your house, in honor of my father."

Samuel smiled. "Agreed," he said.

A few years later, Jesus spoke to his followers.

> *Everyone then who hears these words of mine and acts on them will be like a wise man who built his house on rock. The rain fell, and the floods came and beat on that house, but it did not fall, because it had been founded on rock. And everyone who hears these words of mine and does not act on them will be like a foolish man who built his house on sand. The rain fell and the floods came, and the winds blew and beat against that house, and it fell—and great was its fall.*
>
> **MATTHEW 7:24–27**

REFLECTION

Many of Jesus' parables and sayings have a sense of urgency about them. Now is the time, they say. Drop everything and follow me. Don't think about tomorrow. You must act—today. This story is different. It talks about building a foundation, and this is compared to the one who hears Jesus' words and "acts on them."

Down through the ages, Christians who were serious about following Jesus understood that their lives would change. It would not be easy. Clement of Alexandria in the third century said that Christ, working with the believer, first converts, then disciplines, then imparts wisdom. Others through the centuries have developed different stages or schemas to describe the Christian's spiritual journey. For example, the three stages of the spiritual life have been called the purgative, illuminative, and unitive way. The first, purgative, relates to the need to tame our unruly and wayward nature—to build a solid foundation. The second, illuminative, is the period of learning and practicing what it means to be a Christian. In the third stage, one is more closely connected to God and acts perhaps more freely according to love rather than law.

The relationship to the parable of the house is, of course, that becoming a Christian takes time. A problem can arise when one thinks, *Aha! Now I have arrived at the unitive way. I am with God.* Spiritual pride and self-righteousness, as Jesus often pointed out, are among the worst kinds of evil. The three ways might best be considered as cyclical. We will always need to discipline ourselves; we can always learn more and better practice what it means to live as a Christian, and from time to time we will experience the joy of unity with Christ Our Lord, in God. It takes time and effort to lead a Christian life.

It helps to be in touch with those who came before us. Those of the earliest Christian communities had a sense of the very precious message that had been entrusted to them. The following is from the second-century *Letter to Diognetus.*

> He revealed himself through faith. To faith alone is it given to see God. God, the Ruler and creator of the universe, he who made all things and arranged them in proper order, was man's friend and full of kindness and patience. This he always was, is, and always will be. When he had conceived the great and ineffable thought, he communicated it only to his son. Now, as long as he kept and guarded his wise counsel within himself as a secret, it could appear as if he were not concerned and did not care about us. But he disclosed what he had in mind from the beginning through his beloved son. Through him he revealed it. Thus he granted us all things at once, to share in his blessings, to perceive, and to understand.

PRAYER

Lord Jesus, you were a builder. Help us to build lives based on the love you have given. Help us to clear away the desire for money, the entertainments we chase, the ambition and desire to be noticed. Help us to spend our time and energy on Sacred Scripture. Help us to reach those in need with your healing presence. We know that you are with us and within us. Amen.

QUESTIONS FOR DISCUSSION

1. Do you think it might be true that Joseph was a better carpenter than Jesus? (There is no right answer. The question is meant to help us understand that Jesus was fully human.)
2. How have different practices been helpful to you as you build your life in Christ? Prayer? Spiritual reading? Helping one in need?
3. What times or situations made you think your spiritual world was threatened?
4. What parts of your spiritual "house" need repairs?
5. What do the stages "purgative, illuminative, and unitive" mean to you?
6. Which of these stages do you most often feel like you are in?
7. What are some of the understandings about God that we have received from Jesus Christ?
8. What aspects of God's revelation in Christ are most important to you?

2

The Call of Matthew

WE ARE CALLED

THE CALL OF MATTHEW HAS BEEN FERTILE SOIL FOR THE CHRISTIAN IMAGINATION. It appears, based on the gospels, that Jews of the time hated tax collectors for several reasons. First, they were collaborators, instruments of Rome, earning their pay by joining in the oppression of their countrymen. Second, they seem to have been unsupervised, collecting what they might by guile, threats, or force. It is hard to think of a current equivalent. Perhaps collection agencies that are sometimes ruthless in their tactics have some of the same characteristics. But the repossession of homes and property is, in our day, often bureaucratic and faceless. Then, the tax collectors were real people. But we need not judge. Tax collectors were individuals.

The following conversation takes place a few days after the call of Matthew and the dinner party he gave for Jesus. Aaron, an enthusiastic and talkative partner, sees Matthew approaching and welcomes him in a loud voice.

"Levi, it is good to see you. Wonderful dinner you hosted for the rabbi. We really enjoyed it. But we wondered what happened to you. You are as regular as the rising and setting of the sun. I was worried. You are a rock, an honest businessman, one who knows money and people. Like me, you don't manage all the observances, but we do the best we can.

"Well, I hope you got that mystical rabbi out of your system. We heard you were off with him. Jesus, isn't that his name? He is something. We listened to him. To him, up is down; poor is rich; sad is happy. Who can understand him? Either he is a fake, or he will burn out, or the Romans will nail him to a tree. Anyway, welcome. I do think you could get yourself a better-looking cloak, but there are lots of taxes to be collected. Let's get to work."

Matthew smiled faintly. He liked Aaron. They had been partners in business for a long time. But everything had changed. He spoke quietly, "I just came back to settle a few accounts and sell the rest of my things; then I will join the rabbi Jesus."

Aaron was afraid of this. He spoke in a still-friendly way but more earnestly, "Levi, how are you going to support yourself? You can't drive a nail straight or take the measurements for a house. You have no training as a carpenter, or anything else for that matter. Two hours in the sun and you are exhausted; so you are not a farmer. Will you open a shop? I don't think so. Think, man, you are giving up what you do, and do well. You are an honest tax collector. You do a lot of good in your work. People will miss you."

A hint of a smile remained as Levi/Matthew answered, "He called me. He wants me to help in his work. I never dreamed of such a thing. I am part of his selected group."

"Selected group," interrupted Aaron, "I saw them. We ate with them the other night. They are unschooled and unwashed, mostly fishermen. The rabbi may be a mystic but his judgment in followers, excepting you, of course, is rather—shall we say—questionable. Levi, you have some education. I have seen you reading Greek and Latin as well as Hebrew. You may be a tax collector but you are not like those others of his. The rabbi's followers will drive you crazy or bore you to death."

Matthew answered patiently, "I have spent a few days with them.

They are committed, unshakably bound to the rabbi. They are real, concerned about what he calls the kingdom."

Aaron was concerned. "Yes, I have heard about the kingdom. But what is it? Where is it? Will he raise an army against the Romans? I don't think so, although a few of his followers are known as revolutionaries, and that won't help you. Levi, I guess I can't stop you."

"I can't explain it to you, Aaron," said Matthew, and yet he did try to explain, "Yes, he speaks with stories and sayings that are hard to understand. But he makes us think. He makes us want to see God in new ways—as a Father—and to care for those who are left out and to raise up the lowly. And when we begin to follow his way, we know deep down that it is right and good, that nothing is more important."

"I see there is no changing your mind," Aaron sounded perplexed but resigned. "Listen Levi, you have learning. Write things down. I don't think this rabbi and his followers will amount to anything. But who knows, there may be a good story there."

Matthew hugged his friend, "Yes, well, take care of yourself, Aaron, be honest with the taxes, try to do something for the ones who have trouble paying. Good-bye."

"Good-bye, Levi."

> *After this he went out and saw a tax collector named Levi, sitting at the tax booth; and he said to him, "Follow me." And he got up, left everything and followed him.*
>
> *Then Levi gave a great banquet in his house; and there was a crowd of tax collectors and others sitting at table with him. The Pharisees and their scribes were complaining to his disciples saying, "Why do you eat and drink with tax collectors and sinners?" Jesus answered, "Those who are well have no need of a physician, but those who are sick; I have come to call not the righteous but sinners to repentance."* **LUKE 5:27–32**

REFLECTION

In traditional Catholic thinking, the "Call of Matthew" was proposed as a model of the young man or woman who "left everything" to enter the religious life or seminary. For the religious life, the vows of poverty, chastity, and obedience were seen as the wall separating those who chose to follow in this "more perfect life" from the others who were keeping the commandments and practicing a virtuous Christian life according to their best efforts and insights regarding God's will in their lives. The founders and saints of the religious orders generally did lead lives exhibiting great virtue, and for them the vows did indeed help them to more closely follow Jesus Christ. And more generally, the religious orders often did accomplish important work—in education, the foreign missions, caring for the sick and aged, and other ministries. Some, like the Benedictines and Cistercians (Trappists), devoted themselves exclusively to prayer and work. Diocesan priests, of course, generally were engaged in parish work, particularly administration of the sacraments, and through celibacy and obedience to the bishop were also viewed as different and special.

The theology and spirituality surrounding the Second Vatican Council, as well as other changes, brought new thinking to these areas. All Christians are called as followers of Christ, proceeding on different roads. In addition, a better-educated laity meant that the priest was no longer accepted without question as the highest authority, even in matters of theology, church teaching, and practice.

How does a Catholic think about a "call" from Christ the Lord in today's world? I tried to suggest in the narrative starting this chapter that Matthew may have faced some opposition as he embarked on his new life. Similarly today, one professing Christian belief may face quiet ridicule. And then there is the inner turmoil, the scattered hopes and dreams and fantasies that prevent us from following Jesus more closely. Francis Thomson wrote of the efforts to escape God's call in *The Hound of Heaven*, which starts:

I fled Him, down the nights and down the days;
I fled Him, down the arches of the years;
I fled Him, down the labyrinthine ways
Of my own mind; and in the mist of tears
I hid from Him, and under running laughter.
Up vistaed hopes I sped;
And shot, precipitated,
Adown Titanic glooms of chasmèd fears,
From those strong Feet that followed, followed after.
But with unhurrying chase,
And unperturbèd pace,
Deliberate speed, majestic instancy,
They beat—and a Voice beat
More instant than the Feet—
'All things betray thee, who betrayest Me.'

Do we find God, or does God find us? Yes, God does find us. But in order to find us, each of us, God looks and pursues us. God is there in your life—hidden in plain sight. Try to make time to think, to pray, to look more closely at your life. It may be in your family or personal life; it may be in your work; it may be in your parish or other commitments that Christ is calling you to follow him more closely.

PRAYER

Lord Jesus, I wonder at how you called Matthew. "Follow me," you said. You saw something in him. He saw something in you. Lord, please, you have called me. But please call me again. Help me, like Matthew, to leave the distractions of my work to follow you more closely, more completely. Amen.

QUESTIONS FOR DISCUSSION

1. What surprises you about the ways in which Jesus called his followers?
2. What were those at Matthew's dinner party complaining about?
3. Do you sometimes judge those who are not religiously observant?
4. In what ways do you feel Christ has called you?
5. How have you responded to the call?
6. In what new directions do you think the Church is called to go these days?
7. In what ways do we sometimes avoid or run from God's call?
8. How does God's call come to people in today's world?

3

Peter Tells a Parable

HELPING THE ONES IN OUR PATH

ALBERT NOLAN'S REMARKABLE BOOK, *JESUS BEFORE CHRISTIANITY*, OFFERS RICH INSIGHTS INTO THE HUMAN SIDE OF JESUS. Nolan's understanding of how Jesus lived and taught and even how he thought is based on a careful reading of Scripture combined with an appreciation of the social/historical context. He conjectures that Jesus may have had his own house in Capernaum, which was his base, where he himself entertained and where he shared his life not only with his closest followers but also with those who were rejected, finding themselves beyond the approval of just about everyone. The following is an effort to imagine what a little time might have been like in those days. It is early morning, just after sunrise.

"Andrew, are you awake?" Peter's voice was softer than usual, but easily heard. He was in the bunk next to that of his brother. Several of the other disciples were also there, in the adjoining room. A few others slept outside; it had been a warm evening.

"I am now, Peter."

"Where is the Teacher?"

"Peter, you know that he goes out to pray at night, or very early in the morning. Last night was no different; I heard him go out a few hours ago."

"Why does he do that?"

"Peter, you know what prayer is. At least he has tried to teach us. He is talking with the Father. Where do you think his teachings come from? Anyway, here he comes; ask him."

"Teacher, tell us the story about the man who went down from Jerusalem to Jericho and was all beaten up."

"Peter, let me have a cup of tea, first."

Several of the women who stayed in the house next door came with fresh bread, tea, and fruit. They began to eat.

Peter ate his food quickly, then spoke. "Teacher, let me tell it."

Jesus was eating slowly, "That's a good idea, Peter. Go ahead."

Everyone was quiet as Peter began. He spoke in tones that were both strong and gentle, imitating the way Jesus spoke.

"A man traveled from Jerusalem to Jericho, and on his journey he was beaten by mean and savage robbers who not only took what he had but hit him with large sticks and banged his head against the ground."

"Peter," Jesus interrupted, "What is the point of the story?"

"I'm coming to that, Teacher. It is about the one who showed pity and compassion and was a neighbor."

"Good, so we don't have to overdo the details about the robbers."

"Okay, I'll start over: A certain man went down from Jerusalem to Jericho and on his journey, he fell among robbers who beat him, took his money, and left him by the roadside half dead."

"Good."

"While he was there a useless, hypocritical, money-grubbing priest came by. This priest saw the injured man. You couldn't miss him. But did he stop? Did he show pity? No, like most priests and the rest of those in the temple would do, he passed by."

"Peter."

"I know. But that's what I think when you tell the story, teacher."

"Yes, but..."

"Okay, a priest, seeing him, passed by."

"Good."

"Then a Levite came and, seeing him, passed by."

"Good."

"Then a Samaritan came, and he was actually on an important trip. Well, none of us likes Samaritans very much, but this one was different."

"Peter."

"Then a Samaritan who was on a journey came and, seeing the man, he bound up his wounds and poured in oil to help heal them. And he took him to an inn and gave the innkeeper two pieces of silver and told him to take care of the man and he said, 'On my return trip I will stop and pay you whatever more it might cost.'"

Andrew spoke, "Well told, Peter."

"Thank you," said Peter.

REFLECTION

What does the story of the good Samaritan mean to us, these many centuries later? Of course, we can take it exactly as is. There may be times when we encounter someone who has been badly injured by robbers or others doing grave bodily harm. And we may have the opportunity to help.

But there are other more likely events. Consider a family living in Aleppo while war raged in Syria. There were the parents and five children: A girl of eight, her brother, a year and a half younger, and three younger sisters. The father saw and heard bombing nearby. He told his wife they would have to leave early the next morning. They did and began walking toward Jordan. About an hour later the bombs fell and their home was indeed destroyed. They were able to get a ride and went to Jordan to begin a new life. There they had another child, a girl.

About three years later in a rural town in Connecticut, a group was formed hoping to sponsor a refugee family. The group worked with an organization in New Haven that had developed a workable model for the distribution of tasks in assisting a family with health, education, English learning, housing, etc. A member of the community provided a home on very generous terms.

On August 30, 2016, the family arrived at JFK airport and was met by members of the American group. The following three years kept everyone busy. The group worked hard helping the family adjust in many ways, and we received a great deal in return—as the children learned English and made friends, the father obtained work at a local tea factory, and the mother took care of everything that mothers do, including giving birth and nursing a new baby girl. Then she began to work at a nearby nursing home.

One of my jobs was to work with the father toward his driver's license. He had driven for a number of years in Syria, so driving was not a problem. The difficulty was getting comfortable with the tester and learning enough English to follow the directions. He failed the test five times but was a good sport about it. In the afternoon of one of the tests, I met one of their daughters looking very sad. I asked what the trouble was, and she said, "Daddy didn't win." Eventually he did receive his driver's license and a few very generous people in the community provided funds so he could buy a van.

As a fund raiser, several people worked with the family preparing a supper of Middle Eastern food. About seventy townspeople attended. The food and conversation were good. But the highlight of the evening was when the six children stood on the stage and sang a few songs, concluding with "God Bless America."

Those who engaged in this effort were rewarded many times over in their work with the Syrian family. But we do not offer help in order to gain rewards. Mother Teresa spoke of the dryness, darkness, and loneliness that were so much a part of her life. That she never wavered in her faith and work is both a testimony to her and an encouragement to us. We should be wary of the fleeting "do good" feelings that might accompany our rather meager efforts.

The Samaritan was caring for the alien, the stranger, the immigrant. Caring for "the other" does not come easily to us. But it is encouraged in word and in action throughout the Old and New Testaments. Verses from the Book of Leviticus are particularly strong.

> When an alien resides with you in your land, you shall not oppress the alien. The alien who resides with you shall be to you as the citizen among you; you shall love the alien as yourself, for you were aliens in the land of Egypt. I am the Lord your God. LEVITICUS 19:33–34

Reflecting on this text and on the Book of Ruth, as well as on her own life as an immigrant and as a Christian, Karen Gonzalez writes the following (from *The God Who Sees*, p. 23):

> As an immigrant, I am loved and seen by the holy God of the universe. Our Bible, inspired by God, includes an entire book that deals directly with the just treatment and acceptance of the foreigner. In the many churches I had attended since my childhood, I had never heard that the Scriptures have something to say about the way that immigrants—people like my family and me—should be treated. I had never heard that the Bible commands that we be regarded as native citizens, treated fairly, and even loved like family.

Finally, the First Letter of Peter and a number of early Church documents encourage us as Christians to see ourselves as participants in the public life where we live, but also as aliens: participating but apart. As followers of Christ, we try to separate ourselves from the acquisitiveness and the self-promotion that characterize so much of contemporary life. At the same time, we do not judge. Jesus told us that the different grains grow together. We don't always know who our coworkers are.

PRAYER

God, Our Father, you are the compassionate one. You see all peoples as your children. Why do we so often fail to see others as our brothers and sisters? Help us to recognize your life, your being, and your love in others. Help us to recognize those in need, healing their wounds. You are the father of all.

QUESTIONS FOR DISCUSSION

1. Samaritans were viewed as ethnically different; they were avoided and looked down on. Who are the Samaritans in your world?
2. Who are the immigrants in your world?
3. What can you do for immigrants?
4. How did Jesus act toward non-Jews in his world?
5. In what ways or places do you feel like an immigrant, not accepted?
6. How are immigrants in the United States misjudged?
7. The commentary on the Book of Ruth in the RSV says that, "the values—loyalty, love of family, and generosity toward strangers—are universal." How is this true? When is it not true?
8. Why do we find it difficult to be generous to strangers?
9. What are some of the reasons we should be generous to strangers?

4

Two Centurions

BE SATISFIED?

JESUS' MISSION WAS TO THE PEOPLE OF ISRAEL. But in the gospels there are a number of encounters in which Jesus speaks with the Romans and other Gentiles who occupied their land, or in this case served in the military of Herod Antipas. We are told that John baptized some soldiers. The following incidents are imagined in the lives of two such soldiers.

THE CAST OF CHARACTERS:

Marcus and Lucius: centurions, from Syria, serving Herod Antipas

Antonia: Marcus's wife

Marcus was a strong, well-trained centurion, responsible for about 140 troops, more than the hundred designated by the title. He had spent two years maintaining the peace in Syria, which along with Judea were the two final provinces incorporated into the Roman Empire. Before that he had been stationed in Asia Minor—as it has been traditionally called—which is present-day Turkey. Marcus was always interested in the local religious practices, and particularly the initiation rites. He believed that the Roman Empire was strong and great but also thought there must be something more to life than building roads and temples and sending back huge quantities of grain for those in Rome and the surrounding provinces. He had a wife and two children back in Rome. His friend Lucius, also from Syria, joined him. The life serving Herod turned out to be much the same as what they had been accustomed to. It also made it possible for them to pursue their interest in Judaism. Ultimately they hoped the service might equip them to become Roman citizens. They had even taken Roman names.

Lucius was also a centurion, but unmarried. He was more interested in adventure but had recently fallen for a beautiful young Jewish woman. A day came when both Lucius and Marcus were off duty. They went and listened to the fiery preacher named John. And in a moment of excitement they came forward and John baptized them.

But what did this mean? Had their lives changed? They had to ask him.

> *And the crowds asked him, "What then should we do?" In reply he said to them, "Whoever has two coats must share with anyone who has none; and whoever has food must do likewise." Even tax collectors came to be baptized, and they asked him, "Teacher, what should we do?" He said to them, "Collect no more than the amount prescribed for you." Soldiers also asked him, "And what should we do?" He said to them, "Do not extort money from anyone by threats or false accusations, and be satisfied with your wages."* LUKE 3:10–14

"I don't know," Lucius said, "I don't extort money from people. Well, unless I really need it. And some of these Jews have more money than they know what to do with. And, anyway, it all belongs to us. Emperor Tiberius said so."

"Yes, well, that is the point, I guess." Marcus responded. "This prophet is saying something different. He is saying we should respect these people."

"Yes," Lucius said with a smile. "I respect one in a very big way.

And I would like to do more than respect her. I really do want to marry Rebecca. Do you think the emperor would mind?"

Marcus laughed. "The emperor wouldn't know and as long as you serve as a good centurion, everyone will be happy. Especially since you are a volunteer with Herod."

"Yes, easy for you to say," Lucius responded. "But Rebecca's father cares."

"Well, that is for you to work out," Marcus answered. "But what about being satisfied with your wages? Is that something a prophet should be talking about?"

"No one is satisfied with their wages. Maybe that is what makes him a prophet." Lucius answered.

"Yes, so, what does it mean to be satisfied?" Marcus continued. "Satisfied or not satisfied—does it affect how I live or act. What is really important is whether we get things done. The emperor doesn't care how we feel. He wants us to do our job. Keep order. Win battles. Build roads. Bring back gold and food and all sorts of things to make Rome beautiful. But just maybe being satisfied does make a difference in our lives. I am happy with Antonia, satisfied. And that makes my life better. And when we are not satisfied, I think something bad comes from our hearts and into what we do."

"Well you certainly are turning into a philosopher. And I do love Rebecca. You have to help me get to know her better."

REFLECTION

What would you or I think if our pastor in a sermon said, "Be satisfied with your wages." We might say it's none of the pastor's business, or we might think, what has that got to do with being a good Christian? But John, like Jesus, knew that living in God's love and doing good in our lives starts in the heart and mind and soul. Actions follow. Jesus said more than once that it is what comes from the heart that can soil us.

And it is worth thinking about what it means to be satisfied—with our wages or with many other aspects of our lives. "Satisfied" comes from the Latin word *satis*, which means "enough." It's almost counter-cultural to talk about enough or being satisfied with our pay or our net worth, or with anything. We are told in commercials all day long that we should want more, own more, have more of everything—money, clothes, food, and on and on. But fortunately, there are strong movements against this kind of thinking, as well. Many people are looking for ways to get along with less—to preserve our world in so many ways.

There are further dimensions to this discussion, and there is a lot of history. In 1891 Pope Leo XIII issued the encyclical *Rerum Novarum*. The title comes from the opening words and means "Of New Things." The letter spoke eloquently about justice and the rights of working people to earn enough to live decent lives, taking care of themselves and their families. Since then, Catholic teaching has insisted that there are times when working people should not be satisfied while they are exploited and mistreated and underpaid.

In 1931 Pope Pius XI issued the encyclical *Quadragesimo Anno* (After Forty Years). In it the pope discussed the fact that a great divide had arisen between the worlds of the rich and poor.

> For toward the close of the nineteenth century, the new kind of economic life that had arisen and the new developments of industry had gone to the point in most countries that human society was clearly becoming divided more and more into two classes. One class, very small in number, was enjoying almost all the advantages which modern inventions so abundantly provided; the other, embracing the huge multitude of working people, oppressed by wretched poverty, was vainly seeking escape from the straits wherein it stood.

We can debate whether the gap between the rich and poor has become greater or lesser since those words were written. In any case, millions of people are still exploited, not receiving adequate wages or even the necessities of life. Most of us who are contemplating, reading, and writing about the Christian message are not among the poor and exploited. You and I may be comfortable in the things of this world. But what are we to do about the injustices that leave so many without enough? They cannot be happy if they and their families do not have enough to eat or shelter. We must spread our sense of "enough" to others, to those around us, to the human family.

PRAYER

God our Father, you are the generous one. You have given us this wonderful universe and our earth, the air we breathe, the food we eat. Help us to participate in your generosity. Inspire us to give freely, to help those who do not have enough to eat or enough clothing to wear. Guide us so that we are not selfish and greedy; help us to open our minds and our hearts, and to be generous in every way. Amen.

QUESTIONS FOR DISCUSSION

1. Are you satisfied with your wages?
2. In what ways should we not be satisfied with our earnings?
3. Should the Church be involved with the economics of work and earning?
4. Is our society divided into classes?
5. If so, what can we do about it?
6. How does Jesus' teaching relate to earnings, production, and unions?
7. How did Jesus view his immediate family?
8. How did he view the human family?

5

A Servant

BEYOND ISRAEL

THE CAST OF CHARACTERS:
Marcus and Lucius: as above, centurions
Hector: Marcus's learned Greek slave
Rebecca: the one Lucius loves
Jacob: Rebecca's father

A LOT HAD HAPPENED TO MARCUS AND LUCIUS IN THE FIFTEEN MONTHS SINCE JOHN BAPTIZED THEM. They were both very taken with Judaism. So they used some of their money and also put their troops to work building a synagogue for the town near where they lived. They had not fully converted. But in the readings and in the Jewish people they found wisdom combined with an approach to God as one—creator and guide. It made sense to them more than the multiplicity of arguing, fighting gods of Rome. Yet they remained good soldiers.

Marcus's wife and two children had come to join him, and along with them one of their favorite slaves, Hector. He was a tutor to the children and a good cook for the family. Indeed, his father was Greek but from Israel. Hector spoke several languages and often joined Marcus, who went to listen to Jesus when he could. After Jesus had spoken to the crowds, Hector, who had a wonderful memory, would tell Marcus as much as he could, translating into Latin, and they would talk about what it meant. Marcus was mystified; he knew that Jesus was challenging them to become something more, to do something special, or so he thought. But what was this talk of the kingdom all about? He knew about empires. He was dedicated to protecting the empire of Rome in all its reach. It was his mission at this time of his life.

"Kingdom" as far as he could tell was the same word as "empire," but what Jesus talked about was something else. "The kingdom of God is among you." He could understand that. There is a spark within each of us, and among all of us together, and we must do our best to fan the flames, to awaken our consciences, our sense of duty. When we do that, we also serve the empire that is made from and for all of us. The idea that the Gentiles might enter the kingdom before the children of Israel, well, the gods or God could certainly have their favorites, and these might change. But this idea of somehow giving yourself up: sometimes it sounded as if Jesus wanted his followers to be less—not more—than they were capable of. And the kinds of people Jesus spent his time with! This was troubling. And yet, he kept going to hear Jesus and talking about it. It seemed Jesus was talking to something deep inside Marcus, to a place he himself did not completely understand.

Lucius's life too had changed. He was still very much in love with the young Jewish woman, Rebecca, and spent all the time he could with her. Her father was more lenient to the Romans than many Jews, but he insisted that Lucius become a committed Jew if there were to be any chance at all of his marrying Rebecca.

So Lucius met with Jacob, Rebecca's father, as often as he could. They read the sacred writings and Jacob told Lucius what it all meant. Lucius liked the fact that Jacob was so devoted to learning, to the history of his people, and to finding the right way to live. And the idea of one god above all was not foreign to his way of thinking. He began to think he really could enter into Judaism, and, of course, it would mean he might have a chance to marry Rebecca.

Like Marcus and his slave Hector, Lucius and Jacob discussed the teachings of Jesus. Jacob told Lucius that his people had a long history of prophets—those whose voices called to them to turn away from idols, or selfishness, or becoming like the worldly nations around them. Sometimes, he said, these prophets were killed or at best ignored by most of the people.

"Is that what will become of this Jesus?" Lucius asked. "He seems to have such inner power, and the crowds come to listen. Will it all come to nothing?"

"It is not nothing," Jacob said. "The prophets speak to the spirit. They keep the Lord's message alive. There are always some who hear them. Jesus will die, or be killed, but he is awakening something within the people, within each of us. He is trying to remind us of who we are, of our covenant."

"What is this 'covenant'?" Lucius asked.

"It is an agreement we have with God. It goes back to our father, Abraham, even to Adam." And Jacob told Lucius the stories of Abraham and the promise that he would be the father of a great people and have land on which they would live. Then he told of Moses and the law and the prophets with God's mysterious message.

The next day Marcus and Lucius spent an off day together, something they did less frequently since their lives had changed. They were talking about Jesus.

"He wants to renew the nation," Marcus said. "But some of his ideas are so—." He couldn't find the words. Jesus seemed challenging and a little crazy, caring but in some ways careless. Marcus looked into the distance.

"He is what they call a prophet," Lucius picked up the thread of Marcus's thought. "He wants the people to pay attention to God. In fact, I think he is trying to tell them what God is really like, that God is different from what they think. Very different from what we think."

At that moment, Marcus's wife approached them. It was a beautiful day and they had been sitting on large stones just outside the town. Antonia was very upset as she approached them. She started speaking without even a greeting.

"Hector is sick. It is very bad."

Marcus stood quickly. "What! He was fine yesterday. How can this be? Where is he?"

"It is a fever. He is burning up. His tongue is swollen. He doesn't make sense when he speaks."

They hurried home. It was as Antonia had said. They sent for a doctor, several doctors. Nothing helped.

On the third day Lucius came to visit. Hector seemed to be barely breathing. He woke every hour or so but didn't recognize anyone. He couldn't eat or even drink water. It was clear that he was near death.

Lucius spoke, "This Jesus works wonders. Who knows?"

Marcus was desperate, and he believed in wonders.

"Where is he?" he asked.

"I heard he is returning this way. People will know where to find him."

"How can we bring Hector? The trip might kill him!"

"Perhaps Jesus will come here."

"Perhaps one of his people could go. Would you ask Jacob to ask Jesus on my behalf?" Marcus asked.

"Of course." Lucius answered, and they set out. Marcus remained with Hector.

Jacob and two of the other leaders said they would go and ask Jesus, and as Lucius had said, people along the way had a good idea where to find Jesus. In less than an hour, near sunset, they saw the crowd and recognized some of Jesus' regular followers.

Jacob approached Jesus, respectfully, but his voice showed urgency.

"Rabbi, there is a centurion whose servant is near death. He has been good to our people, even building a synagogue; will you heal him?"

"Let us go to him," Jesus said simply, and they began to walk in the direction of Marcus's home. Some boys ran on ahead, anxious to carry news of what was happening. They found Marcus pacing outside his home and told him that Jesus was coming. Marcus was happy but also felt an overwhelming sense of—it was difficult to identify. He felt his usual confidence as a Roman centurion, but it was mixed with respect and awe at this teacher who held power and authority in different ways. He immediately went next door and asked the father of one of the boys to go quickly and greet the rabbi Jesus, and he told him exactly what to say.

This neighbor and friend, Noah, left immediately with the boys and several other neighbors. They found Jesus and the crowd entering the town. They spoke to him in the words Marcus had given them.

> After Jesus had finished all his sayings in the hearing of the people, he entered Capernaum. A centurion there had a slave whom he valued highly, and who was ill and close to death. When he heard about Jesus, he sent some Jewish elders to him, asking him to come and heal his slave. When they came to Jesus they appealed to him earnestly, saying, "He is worthy of having you do this for him, for he loves our people, and it is he who built our synagogue for us. And Jesus went with them, but when he was not far from the house the centurion sent friends to say to him, "Lord, do not trouble yourself, for I am not worthy to have you come under my roof, therefore I did not presume to come to you. But only speak the word, and let my servant be healed. For I also am a man set under authority, with soldiers under me, and I say to one, 'Go,' and he goes, and to another, 'Come,' and he comes, and to my slave, 'Do this,' and the slave does it." When Jesus heard this he was amazed at him, and turning to the crowd that followed him, he said, "I tell you, not even in Israel, have I found such faith." When those who had been sent returned to the house, they found the slave in good health. LUKE 7:1–10

REFLECTION

What was it that attracted those first-century Greeks and Romans to the Christian faith, to believe in Christ, and to attach themselves to a community that transcends the grip of state, ethnicity, and family? Like those in the Scripture passage above, they found something in the person, teaching, and total giving-life of Jesus that led them to him and bound them together in new ways. The second-century document mentioned earlier, *Letter to Diognetus*, discusses the beliefs and practices of the early Christians. We do not know the author of this document, and perhaps this is fitting, as you will see from the following excerpt, describing Christian life.

> They live in Greek cities and they live in non-Greek cities according to the lot of each one. They conform to the customs of their country in dress, food, and the general mode of life, and yet they show a remarkable, an admittedly extraordinary structure of their own life together. They live in their own countries, but only as guests and aliens. They take part in everything as citizens and endure everything as aliens. Every foreign country is their homeland, and every homeland is a foreign country to them.

For those first Christians, the faith encompassed everything. Believing in Christ meant accepting his view of the world, his way of doing things. Now these two thousand years later, we have a tendency to fit our faith into the broad framework of our lives.

Is there a danger in giving one's allegiance too much to the nation? Does love of country lead us to devalue, ignore, and mistrust those of other nations and ethnicities? Is our self-centeredness as a people directly contrary to what Jesus is telling us—in the parable of the good Samaritan, in his criticisms of the religious leaders of his own tradition? As we become comfortable in our nationality or ethnicity, do we betray Christ, who stands for and stands within every person?

We should not only stand with and stand for the strangers in our midst; we should be aliens in our own land.

PRAYER

God, you are the Father of all, and yet we, as followers of Jesus, your Son, give ourselves to you in a special way. Help us to be in this world, working with people of all nations and beliefs, but also recognizing that we follow Jesus in a special way. Send your Holy Spirit among us to help us see you in wour neighbors and serve you in our brothers and sisters. Amen.

QUESTIONS FOR DISCUSSION

1. How does it seem that Jesus viewed his mission to those beyond Israel?
2. What is the evidence that Jesus saw his work as extending beyond Israel?
3. What was it that attracted the Romans to Jesus?
4. What does the *Letter to Diognetus* mean about the Christians participating in the life and customs but only as strangers?
5. What might have been some of the things in which the first Christians did not participate?
6. How do you feel about giving your allegiance to your country?
7. How might patriotism conflict with Christianity?
8. Where do you think Jesus stands with regard to different nations?

6

Conversation on the Road

SOUL AND BODY TOGETHER

THE FOLLOWING TAKES PLACE AFTER PETER, JAMES, AND JOHN WERE TAKEN UP A MOUNTAIN TO WITNESS JESUS TRANSFIGURED. They had seen his glory, accompanied by Moses and Elijah, and yet were quick to return to their everyday concerns. When Jesus tells his followers they must become like little children, it is not so much that children are docile and innocent as that they were, in Jesus' time, insignificant. Children were part of everyday life in ancient Israel, probably always around, so it was easy for Jesus to reach out and hold a child. And although parents loved their children, cared for them, and grieved when they became sick or died, as we do, there was a difference—the parents in first-century Israel did not dote on their children. In fact, children did not have any rights of their own; they were the property of their parents. It was likely that parents gave them work to do at an early age, and this work increased as they grew. (The father of the Syrian family in our town told me that when he was eight years old his father told him he would have to stop school and work with him, and so as a child he began to work with his father.) So for the disciples to become like children meant losing something of their identity, as Jesus taught in other ways: You must lose your life in order to find it.

It was a cool, overcast day, and the weather suited the mood of Jesus' followers. Jesus walked alone, in front, head slightly bowed, deep in thought and prayer. Behind him, Peter, James, and John walked, then the rest of the twelve, other followers, the women who helped, and there were always others who followed for a few hours, hoping for a miracle or sign.

Peter spoke, "Have you ever seen someone crucified?"

James answered, "What kind of a question is that? You know we've all seen people crucified. They are done in public. We saw several last year after the insurrection."

Peter responded, "I guess I meant have you ever seen someone you know well on a cross? Did it ever occur to you that it could happen to us, to you?"

John intervened, "Peter, we are not turning back. You know that. We have been called to something we don't really understand. But the Lord we follow deserves our complete trust. And we have seen him in his glory. We know that the victory will be his. Let's talk about him. What is it in him that most attracts and engages you?"

Peter thought for a short time, but longer than he usually did, before responding. "He has a way of knowing each of us in a special way. He knows that I am too quick, so he asks me questions to make me think. He selected Matthew, of all people, hardly knowing him. We knew that Matthew was different from most of the tax collectors—honest and kind—I mean I knew him a little bit. But to select him to be with us—none of us would have thought that was a good idea. And the people who are sick or with demons—he approaches them, talks to them, touches them. He even listens to the Romans when they come to him. He accepts the women. I think what I see most is this ability to take each of us in our own lives and let us see new things that we never imagined."

They walked silently for a few minutes, each thinking of Peter's words and how the Lord had chosen them—each as an individual—and how he was making them into something more, as community.

Peter spoke, "James, what is most important to you in the Lord?"

James also thought for a moment, then he spoke. "The way he teaches is most amazing. His stories and sayings are mysterious, but they reach deeply into our hearts. He tells people, 'Hearing you do not hear, and seeing you do not see.' What can that mean? And yet we know what it means. The Spirit of God can be found, or completely missed, in his words, in the Writings, in the world around us, and in people. 'Don't hide your light.' He encourages us to be something more—to try to be like him. And we could think about his stories forever. Imagine the father waiting for his son who went off and squandered his inheritance—could we deal with our children like that? I spend all my time thinking about what he says."

James turned to his brother, "John, what about you?"

John had been listening and was ready to speak. "Of course, I agree with both of you. The Lord's way of encountering people and his words—both draw us to him, and even beyond. But what is it that makes him live within us? It is love. He carries it with him and pours it out among us. He pours God's love—on Magdala, on children, on Gentiles. We don't always understand it, but God is with us."

"But let me ask another question," John continued. "What is it that is the most difficult to understand?"

Peter and James answered with one voice, "The kingdom."

"Yes," said John, "I agree. What does he mean by 'the kingdom'?"

Peter spoke, "We have to get rid of the Romans and then bring back the glory of the nation. Israel will again take its place among the peoples of the world. Jesus will be our king."

"And I," James said, "will be his general, leading the army of the nation. I will be at his right hand."

"You?" Peter said, "Why you? You know he wants me as the leader of us all. I will be his emissary to all the other nations. I will be the one he trusts most."

John spoke quietly, "You know he talks to me about things that concern him most. I will be his most intimate counselor."

Andrew and some of the others overheard this last conversation and joined in, protesting that each of them had claim to a special relationship with the Lord, in fact to be most important in his kingdom. Their voices became louder as they argued. They reached a town, and while arrangements were being made for a meal, Jesus joined them.

> *Then they came to Capernaum; and when he was in the house he asked them, "What were you arguing about on the way?" But they were silent, for on the way they had argued with one another about who was the greatest. He sat down, called the twelve, and said to them, "Whoever wants to be first must be last of all and servant of all." Then he took a little child and put it among them; and taking it in his arms, he said to them, "Whoever welcomes one such child in my name welcomes me and whoever welcomes me welcomes not me but the one who sent me."* **MARK 9:33–37**

REFLECTION

It was not really until his life was complete that the followers of Jesus were able to grasp his teachings and follow his example. That example teaches about the paradoxes of living the Christian life and must reflect the paradoxes that Jesus taught and lived. We are to live with the simplicity of children and yet be ready for whatever difficulty life might bring. The early Christians saw themselves to be carrying out a wonderful, world-changing mission. They were bringing a new order of things, and they were doing it by turning their backs on power, prestige, and treasure. Again, the *Letter to Diognetus* gives insights to help our meditation.

> In a word: what the soul is in the body, the Christians are in the world. As the soul is present in all the members of the body, so Christians are present in all the cities of the world. As the soul lives in the body, yet does not have its origin in the body, so the Christians live in the world yet are not of the world. Invisible, the soul is enclosed by the visible body.

For philosophers and theologians through the ages, the word "soul" meant the non-material, immortal, life-giving principle that directs the body. In modern times, the meaning of "soul" has broadened. It now often refers to the energy that one brings to a task or to life itself. In a way this relates back to the Scriptures in which God breathes, and that breath becomes the spirit-giving life to the person.

The selection quoted above goes on to say that the soul loves the body but the body hates the soul. We might consider this more as a poetic than a philosophical expression. Christians (the soul) love the world (the body) because it has been created by God and redeemed by Christ. But the world, with all its impulses, greed, and selfishness, does not like the constraints that Christianity requires.

The questions continue—in each of us and in Christianity—about how the Christian community should relate to the world of politics, business, entertainment, and all the rest. It is not enough for us to compartmentalize—in effect being Christians when we are in church or participating in church-related activities. We must enter into government and business with all the muck and the disappointments. As the soul energizes and leads the body, so we as Christians must lead the way—from within. What this means will be different for each of us and the demands will vary at different times and places, but the Spirit is with us, guiding and directing.

PRAYER

Lord Jesus, we thank you for the great works you accomplished when you walked the earth, for your teachings that inspire and instruct us, and for the love you brought. Help us imitate you, to live by your guidance, to accept your love, and to bring it to others. Amen.

QUESTIONS FOR DISCUSSION

1. What do you find most appealing about Jesus?
2. What to you is most mysterious about Jesus?
3. What to you is difficult about living as a Christian?
4. What might it mean to say that Christians are the soul of the world?
5. How is our view of Christianity different from that of the earliest Christians?
6. How might we be compromised by our work?
7. How might our family life compromise our Christian living?
8. Is Christianity in any way the soul of your community?

7

Jesus with Friends

HAPPINESS

JESUS NEEDED THE WARMTH OF HUMAN FRIENDSHIP JUST AS WE DO. And he had friends with whom he visited and talked. We don't know a lot about these visits and conversations. And so our imaginations fill in.

It was about an hour before sunset, a warm and quiet evening. Jesus was alone as he approached the door of his friends' house. Being alone was unusual for Jesus—in view of the time of day, the activities of recent days, and simply because of the life he chose to live. But he was indeed alone as he knocked on the door. He heard a voice from within, "Come in, please, the door is not barred." He opened the door and walked through the front room to the cooking and eating area. Martha was kneading a large mound of dough. It would be enough for at least six loaves of bread, Jesus thought.

"Yeshua!" Martha exclaimed, "I didn't know it was you. I would have come to the door."

"It is all right," Jesus responded, "I know you are generally busy at work."

"Busy is right," said Martha, "I won't say I'm the only one who works around here, but... well we have been through that before.

Lazarus and Mary are out walking. Are Peter and the others on the way?"

"No, I told them to go and visit their families and friends for a few days."

Martha was surprised, "Really, why is that?"

"It will be good for them and for their families. Peter, for one, needs to go fishing from time to time. John and James could help their father, who is not very well. And the others—well, it will be good for all of them."

"And for you?" Martha asked.

"Yes, for me as well." Jesus answered, with a hint of a smile.

"May I ask you something?" Martha asked.

"Of course."

"Today," Martha was hesitant, "This afternoon, did you know my brother would come out when you called? Did you know for certain?"

"Yes, Martha, I knew." Jesus said quietly.

"But," Martha continued, "how could you. I mean…it is so strange. He was dead, wasn't he?'

"Yes," Jesus answered, "Lazarus was dead, and I suppose it seems surprising and strange. But isn't it surprising and wonderful how the leaven makes the dough rise and it becomes bread, or how a seed can turn into a flower or a tree?"

"Yes," Martha responded, "These things are wonderful, but they happen every day. And we understand what happens—in a way. And my cooking is not a miracle."

"Well, yes," said Jesus, "We do understand some of these things. But what seems to me much more difficult to understand than someone returning to life is that a man, a person, could take life away from another. How is that possible? How can people, even nations, rise up and kill, destroy one another? Kill me, perhaps. I know our own nation has a long history of this. But when you stop to think, isn't this—killing—just as difficult to understand as bringing someone back from the dead?"

Jesus seemed distressed. Martha spoke quietly, "Yes, I never—I never thought of it that way."

> *Then Jesus, again greatly disturbed, came to the tomb. It was a cave, and a stone was lying against it. Jesus said, "Take away the stone." Martha, the sister of the dead man, said to him, "Lord, already there is a stench because he has been dead four days." Jesus said to her, "Did I not tell you that if you believed, you would see the glory of God?" So they took away the stone. And Jesus looked upward and said, "Father, I thank you for having heard me. I know that you always hear me, but I have said this for the sake of the crowd standing here, so that they may believe that you sent me." When he had said this, he cried with a loud voice, "Lazarus, come out!" The dead man came out, his hands and feet bound with strips of cloth, and his face wrapped in a cloth. Jesus said to them, "Unbind him, and let him go."* **JOHN 11:38–44**

REFLECTION

Some have said that in curing the sick and bringing life back to those who had been dead, Jesus proved his divinity. The argument goes that Jesus said he was divine, and he proved it. I think we might look at it another way. We who already believe that Jesus was and is fully human and fully divine—based on the totality of his life, teaching, works, death, and resurrection—see him bringing the limitless love and compassion of God to everything he does.

Jesus healed because the suffering touched his heart. We read above that Jesus was "greatly disturbed." This was because Lazarus, his dear friend, was dead. Can we in some way participate in the compassion that Jesus brought to this world? We can and we must. Suffering is universal, and compassion means "to suffer with." And compassion is needed in today's world.

We cannot heal as Jesus did, but we can help care for those who are ill. People are living longer than ever, and the final years of many are difficult, as the body, mind, and sometimes even the spirit seem to decline. Even doctors are often not prepared to help their patients face the end. There are, however, teams in some hospitals engaged in what is called palliative care. They work to help those in the final stages of life, along with their families and friends, discuss what is best as the end approaches.

Perhaps in some ways this is what Jesus was doing. In his compassion he was suffering with those he encountered but also easing their pain. And he sensed that his own life would not last much longer. We in our own way can imitate and join with him in helping those around us, taking into ourselves some of their pain. We have relatives and friends who are suffering. They need our help: bringing a meal, making a call, visiting. The young and old are meant to be together—to share life.

The writings of the earliest Christians are again helpful to us as we try to bring God's compassion to those in need. Again, from the *Letter to Diognetus*:

> Happiness does not consist in ruling over one's neighbors or in longing to have more than one's weaker fellowmen. Nor does it consist in being rich and in oppressing those lowlier than oneself. No one can imitate God by doing such things. They are alien to his sublimity. On the contrary, anyone who takes his neighbor's burden upon himself, who tries to help the weaker one in points where he has an advantage, who give what he has received from God to those who need it, takes God's place, as it were, in the eyes of those who receive. He is an imitator of God.

PRAYER

Lord Jesus, we wonder at your mercy, your power, and your compassion. You suffered with Lazarus, and you suffer with us. None of us knows the day or hour of death. We are frightened by the thought of the end. But we trust that you are with us and will be with us. Help us to be with one another, to suffer with one another, as we prepare for the end of this life. Be with us. Amen.

QUESTIONS FOR DISCUSSION

1. Do you think Jesus may have needed the warmth of human friendship?
2. Does the imaginative incident seem reasonable or possible? Why or why not?
3. Why do you think Jesus was "greatly disturbed"?
4. What have you learned about the life that Jesus shared with the Father?
5. How does that life affect us?
6. Do some people try to find happiness in riches and by oppressing others?
7. How can you take your neighbor's burden on yourself?
8. How can we participate in the compassion of Jesus?

8

Judas

THE DIVIDED MIND

Jesus chose Judas Iscariot as one of the Twelve. Judas kept the common purse and complained about the woman wasting precious oil by pouring it over Jesus' feet, saying it might have been sold and the money given to the poor. He said this, the gospel tells us, not out of concern for the poor but because he was a thief. Jesus stated a number of times that he would be betrayed, and at the Last Supper, Jesus made it clear that Judas was the one. Later that night Judas came, leading a group of temple guards, and identified Jesus with a kiss. The following takes place sometime before that night.

The high priest smiled, warmly, he hoped, and spoke, "Good morning, Judas."

Judas answered, "You sent for me?"

The high priest demurred, "Not sent for you. I just wanted to talk. I knew your father, knew you when you were a boy, remember? So how are you now? How are things with this rabbi of yours, this Jesus? What kind of man is he?"

Judas looked at the high priest, then at the sky, then at the ground. He waited a minute and then spoke slowly. "What kind of man is Jesus? Sometimes I think I know. Then I don't know. I thought he might be the one to lead us to something big, throw off the Romans, at least harass them, make life difficult for them. Peter is strong; he will fight. But Jesus—it's not what he wants. He talks about loving our enemies, doing good to those who hate us, turning the other cheek; I don't know what it's all about. He doesn't seem to care for our own customs."

The high priest pursued this. "That's the thing. We have no quarrel with rabbis. They are important. But we have laws and customs; they make us what we are. Lose these, and where are we? Could you help us with this Jesus?"

"Help you?"

"We need to talk with him, question him, help him see what he is doing to the nation."

Judas was attentive, "Why do you need me?"

"The crowds. You never know. One day, he is with a small group. The next day, he is with five thousand people. The crowds are fickle. We don't want a riot, violence. We have enough trouble with the Romans. You can help us. Just take a few of the temple guards, some quiet night."

"What would you do with him? Would you beat him?"

"No more than the law prescribes. We want to encourage him to do what is best for the nation, for all of us. We know you haven't worked for a few years. We can pay for your service. As much as thirty pieces of silver."

"That's a lot."

The high priest spoke quietly. "You could use the money. I heard you keep the purse for the group. How is that?"

Judas was confused. "How is it? Sometimes people give us money—for food, for what we need. Half the time Jesus tells me to give it to the poor. I try to keep some aside, you know for the group, even for myself, in case.... It's not very well run. I could use some money, especially if I leave the group or if the whole thing falls apart."

"Of course, you could."

"You wouldn't give him to the Romans?"

"Why should we do that? This is our business."

Judas thought out loud. "The Passover is coming. People will be at home, preparing for the celebration."

"My thought exactly. Could happen the day after tomorrow. Here is the money."

"I will come for your men, sunset Thursday."

"Good man, Judas, you won't regret this."

> *When Judas, his betrayer, saw that Jesus was condemned, he repented and brought back the thirty pieces of silver to the chief priests and the elders. He said, "I have sinned by betraying innocent blood." But they said, "What is that to us? See to it yourself." Throwing down the pieces of silver in the temple, he departed and he went and hanged himself.*
>
> **MATTHEW 27:3–5**

REFLECTION

Jesus was gentle and compassionate but also uncompromising in his life and in his message. It seems he had no need or use for money. He had extraordinary love and concern for the poor. He preached full commitment—not necessarily the same for each person but still uncompromising.

We don't know very much about Judas. The gospels say that he was in charge of the money and sometimes helped himself. Did Jesus choose him knowing that he would be the betrayer. This has been said, but I don't think so. We see weaknesses in a number of the Twelve. And Judas did indeed repent. It is certainly not for us to judge. But perhaps we can learn something. Judas was attracted to Jesus, but he was also drawn to money.

The fathers of the church warned against being "double minded." They rightly understood that Jesus expected total commitment from his followers. Christians of every age have recognized this. But the message must be learned anew by each age of Christians. We ourselves in this age of multitasking are happy to be going in several directions all the time. But double-mindedness is a danger to our faith. Another early Christian document, *The Shepherd of Hermas*, puts it this way:

> The angel of righteousness is delicate and modest, meek and even-tempered. When she rises up in your heart, immediately she speaks with you about righteousness, self-control, and every just work and glorious virtue. Look now at the angel of iniquity. First of all, she is sharp-tempered, sour and unreasonable. When she rises up in your heart, you will know of her presence from her works.

As with Judas in our brief imaginative exercise above, we often try to minimize the possible effects of evil when we are on the brink. We may not want to look squarely at where this is leading. It might be a source of money, a new friendship, an idle occupation, or a full-time job. We can look at the "innocent" side. The benefits in terms of money or pleasure may be modest. Everyone does this sort of thing. I leave it for you to examine carefully where this new situation or temptation might be coming from and where it might be leading your life.

There are also those good angels always calling to us. It may be inconvenient, or it may cost a bit one way or another. It may not be easy to pray and meditate for thirty minutes. But if you let these angels speak to you, there will be a deep-down knowledge, joy, and satisfaction. Your life in God will grow.

PRAYER

Come Holy Spirit, guide my thinking, my feelings, my decisions. Help us all, as followers of Jesus, to give fully. Help us not to be divided, holding back some of our love. Help us not to give any part of ourselves to money, to idle pleasures, making ourselves look special. Help us give ourselves fully to God, our Father, through Christ, our Lord. Amen.

QUESTIONS FOR DISCUSSION

1. Why do you think Jesus chose Judas as one of the Twelve?
2. Why do you think Jesus put Judas in charge of the money?
3. How do you understand the "double mind"?
4. How have you experienced the double mind?
5. How do we sometimes try to explain away the evil within us?
6. How should we try to overcome the spirit of evil?
7. How are good and evil intertwined in today's world?
8. How have your good angels helped you avoid evil?

9

An Arrest and Trial

TESTING FAITH

Due to shortages in military personnel, Pilate had borrowed some of the centurions from Herod. Marcus and Lucius were among them. Marcus arrived at the garrison where Lucius was stationed. It was night. "They have arrested Jesus, taken him for questioning, and then sent him to Pilate. It's not good."

Lucius answered, his face and voice mirroring the grim Marcus. "I heard. He has been to the Jewish leaders. Lucentius is the centurion on duty. He has a mean streak. And some of his men are much worse."

Marcus answered, "Who is on tomorrow?"

"I am," Lucius said.

"Let's go," Marcus said.

The Romans kept strict regulations about changing centurions and cohorts. At just a few minutes before sunrise, Lucius and Marcus arrived at Pilate's compound. Lucius saluted Lucentius, who then left with his cohort. Like Roman soldiers everywhere, Lucius and Marcus had witnessed and taken part in beatings and crucifixions. What they saw was not new but the level of brutality and its aftereffects were different. Jesus had been badly beaten. He sat alone. His figure was one of resignation and acceptance, but the pain was evident. He looked at Marcus.

"How is your servant?" he asked.

"He owes his life to you and has used it well since his recovery. He follows your way," Marcus answered.

"That is good," Jesus responded.

"Let me do something about those thorns," Marcus said, trying gently to remove the mockery of a crown.

"Leave it," Jesus said. "It is meant to be."

Marcus accepted what he was told. They brought Jesus a little water. He was too weak to say very much, but the two centurions sat nearby and couldn't refrain from asking a few questions. Lucius wanted to know about the prophets, and Jesus explained their vision of a new world and told them more about the kingdom. They understood a little; their hearts were yearning for more. Jesus told them that his work was just beginning. They could be part of it.

"You can't escape," Marcus said. "Even we couldn't manage that. It all depends on Pilate. Your work may be over."

"Try to believe," Jesus said. "In my death, new life will come—for me and you."

They had grown in their admiration of Jesus, but this was pushing their understanding; they knew deep down that at some point they had to cross a bridge from understanding to faith. They asked Jesus if there was anything more they could do for him. He said no, and they sat in silent vigil.

Pilate sent for Jesus, tried weakly to release him, weakly condemned him, and the crucifixion began. Lucius did what he could, conscripting someone to help carry the cross. The crucifixion itself was routine in one way, horrific in another. As soldiers drove nails into the body of Jesus, Lucius and Marcus suddenly felt what Jesus must have been trying to tell them: that his spirit of love is within all of us. Beyond that, their grief was mixed with duty to get it done.

> *It was now about noon, and darkness came over the whole land until three in the afternoon, while the sun's light failed,*

and the curtain of the temple was torn in two. Then Jesus, crying with a loud voice, said, "Father, into your hands I commend my spirit." Having said this, he breathed his last. When the centurion saw what had taken place, he praised God and said, "Certainly this man was innocent." And when all the crowds who had gathered there for this spectacle saw what had taken place, they returned home, beating their breasts. But all his acquaintances, including the women who had followed him from Galilee, stood at a distance, watching these things. **LUKE 23:44–49**

REFLECTION

Confronted with the suffering and death of Jesus Christ Our Lord, our best response is prayer. One of the most beautiful prayers for this purpose is that of the *Canons of Hyppolytus,* which was written in the third or fourth century and invites us to pray with Jesus. The prayer is a kind of early creed, liturgy, and confessional document of great warmth and beauty.

> We thank thee, O God, through thy beloved servant, Jesus Christ. Thou didst send him to us in these last days, a healing savior and redeemer, and the messenger of thy will. Thou didst make all things through him, the Logos, proceeding from thee. In him thou art rejoicing. From heaven thou didst send him into the virgin's womb. Dwelling within her, he became flesh, was manifested as thy son, born of the Holy Spirit and the virgin. He fulfilled thy will and prepared a holy people for thee. He spread out his hands when he suffered so that he might set free from suffering those who trusted in thee.

It takes time and effort to nourish our lives of faith. Time and effort are needed in our personal lives. Building a marriage, a family, friendships—these things take time. And it is the same with our spiritual lives and journeys. We must spend time reading and studying; we must pray earnestly, whether we feel like it or not. We must help those in need—the poor, those who are left out. If we don't work at these things, our house may indeed fall when hard times come. What are the storms that threaten our spiritual well-being? They are different for each of us and at different times of life.

And the storms do come. Christ, Our Lord, was himself tested more than we can bear to contemplate. For us, faith always faces challenges and is mixed with doubt. How much of the Bible is to be taken literally? Why is there so much evil and wanton destruction in the world around us? Why am I so mean to those who love me? So shortsighted and weak-willed in what I ought to do?

And what about Jesus as God? What does this mean? This is the ultimate "not possible" for the sophisticated modern person. The Greeks and Romans told stories about people and gods having children together. But we are beyond that. We live in a world that extends for billions of years in time and billions of light years in space. Are we supposed to believe that a rather insignificant carpenter—yes, and a remarkable teacher with an extraordinary vision of things, but who like all of us lived for only a few years—had and has a share in the eternal Godhead? Yes, that is what we believe.

Those who study the universe tell us that about thirteen billion years ago, it all began from a very, very small—something—a singularity they call it, because it was before the normal laws of space and time, matter and energy were at work. From that small—we might even say insignificant—beginning came the vast and multiform universe in which we live. How did it happen? What happened?

In the same way, Jesus Christ was and is indeed a singularity. He stretches our minds and hearts, our faith and love—far beyond the here and now. He was and is in touch with the God and power who created and sustains the universe and all that is within it. We give ourselves in faith, and yet we struggle with this thinking, this belief.

PRAYER

Lord Jesus Christ, we are witnesses to your patient suffering. We believe with the faith given to us that in submitting to the powers of the world you released the power of love and forgiveness among all peoples. What you did lets us see all people as our brothers and sisters—this is what you died for, that we might be one with you and with one another.

QUESTIONS FOR DISCUSSION

1. How might the crucifixion of Jesus test your faith?
2. How is the crucifixion consoling?
3. What might Jesus' followers have been thinking at his crucifixion?
4. What messages do we take from the crucifixion?
5. Does belief in Jesus' divinity test your faith?
6. In what ways does the Bible test your faith?
7. What do you say in prayer when you contemplate the crucifixion?
8. What parts of our faith do you find most difficult?

10

Alive

WOMEN IN THE CHURCH

MARY MAGDALENE, JOANNA, AND ANOTHER WOMAN NAMED MARY HAD HELPED PREPARE JESUS' BODY, cleaning off the blood as well as they could and wrapping the body in burial cloth. They went with a small group, including Jesus' mother, to the tomb that had been donated. Then they talked and quietly cried through the night. During the following day they talked about all the things Jesus had said and done.

Very early the next morning they came together again.

"I'm so afraid," said Mary Magdalene. "What if they return?"

"The demons?" asked Joanna.

"Yes, the demons. Jesus drove them out, but I always thought I had to stay near him. He brought peace to my heart and it stayed. But now I am afraid. How will we live without him?"

Joanna's heart ached for Mary, "Do you remember when we were near the town of Nain and the woman whose only son had died was weeping, and Jesus was filled with compassion and he took the young man's hand and told him to arise. Then the man did arise, and Jesus gave him to his mother, almost like he was introducing them. It was beautiful."

"Yes," said Mary. "I remember. But why would they kill him?"

"Who can understand it?" Joanna continued. "Remember the first time we went with him to his hometown and they wouldn't listen. They nearly killed Jesus. And all he said was that prophets are not honored in their own country."

"Yes," Mary replied. "But why did God permit such a thing?"

The other Mary spoke quietly. "Remember what Isaiah said,

> *Upon him was the punishment that made us whole*
> *And by his bruises we are all healed.*
> *All we like sheep have gone astray;*
> *We have all turned to our own way,*
> *And the Lord has laid on him the iniquity of us all.*
>
> **ISAIAH 53:5–6**

Mary Magdalene spoke, "Yes we have all done evil. Will this make us right with God? I am going to the tomb."

"I will come too."

> *After the Sabbath, as the first day of the week was dawning, Mary Magdalene and the other Mary went to the tomb. And suddenly there was a great earthquake, for an angel of the Lord, descending from heaven, came and rolled back the stone and sat on it. His appearance was like lightning, and his clothing white as snow. For fear of him the guards shook and became like dead men. But the angel said to the women, "Do not be afraid, I know that you are looking for Jesus who was crucified. He is not here, for he has been raised, as he said."*
>
> **MATTHEW 28:1–6**

REFLECTION

In the gospel accounts it is Mary Magdalene who alone or with others is among the first to find the empty tomb; and she alone or with others encounters the risen Jesus. Is this an accident that just by chance she and the other women were the ones? Or is there some very important message here—for us, about women?

Jesus chose men as the Twelve, representing new leadership and representing the twelve tribes of Israel. The history of Israel was patriarchal, built on men, so, of course, Jesus would select men to represent the new kingdom. But now in his new life everything is different.

Women were very active in the early Christian communities, as described in the letters of Paul and the Acts of the Apostles. In his letter to the Romans Paul greets Priscilla, a woman, and Aquila, a man, and the church that meets in their house, meaning they likely, together or separately, presided at the Lord's Supper. We would call them priests.

Over the centuries, it seems, cultural forces produced the male-dominated church in which we find ourselves. In recent years, however, things have been changing, most notably in the Protestant churches where women are now ordained and are serving as competent and inspiring pastors. The Catholic Church is, of course, moving more slowly. An excellent book, *Catholic Women Speak,* is filled with thoughts about where we are and where we might be headed. One idea worthy of meditation and action is that man and woman together make up the image of God, and therefore marginalizing women distorts the image of God among us.

Jesus called on God as father. But he talked and taught about this father as one with unconditional love, one who welcomed back the sinner no matter what. We need to introduce the feelings of mother into our sense of who God is. And women can help us with this.

The Catholic novelist Alice McDermott addresses the issue in uncompromising terms.

No Christian should need to be reminded of the moral error of discrimination. We hold at the center of our faith the belief that every human life is of equal value. And yet the Roman Catholic Church, my church, excludes more than half its members from full participation by barring women, for reasons of gender alone, from the priesthood.

The moral consequences of this failing become abundantly clear each time another instance of clergy abuse, and cover-up, is revealed. It is the inevitable logic of discrimination: If one life, one person, is of more value than another, then "the other," the lesser, is dispensable. For the male leaders of the Catholic Church, the lives of women and children become secondary to the concerns of the more worthy, the more powerful, the more essential person—the male person, themselves.

The Catholic Church needs to correct this moral error.

In two gospel accounts, Mary Magdalene is the first witness to the resurrection. She is the messenger who goes to the others; that is why she is called the apostle to the apostles. Jesus instructed her, "Go tell my brothers." Somehow, we have lost this spirit—the recognition that women receive and pass along God's message in a very special way—the revelation that Christ is alive and with and within all of us.

PRAYER

Lord God, you are our Father and also our Mother. Send your Holy Spirit to enlighten our minds and warm our hearts so that we may understand that no organization, no community, no church can be complete until women participate in a way equal to men. Guide and help us to live and act as one people.

QUESTIONS FOR DISCUSSION

1. What has been the role of women in the parishes you have attended?
2. What do you think about Jesus appearing to Mary Magdalene?
3. How and why have women been left out over the centuries?
4. What is changing?
5. What will it take for women to participate fully in the church?
6. What do you think about the emotion expressed by Alice McDermott?
7. What women in history have inspired you?
8. What women have personally helped you grow as a Christian?

11

Peter Preaching

REPENTANCE AND FREEDOM

THE WEEKS AFTER THE CRUCIFIXION OF JESUS HAD BEEN BUSY AND TIRING FOR MARCUS. Pilate did not want trouble, certainly not an insurrection, but he also did not want to fan the flames by harassing people or taking prisoners unnecessarily. So he put Marcus in charge of watching, listening, and finding out what was going on. It was not the kind of work Marcus liked.

The crucifixion disturbed Marcus. Jesus was clearly an innocent man. More than that, he was a man of vision, a prophet, as they say in this land. Marcus didn't know what he was hoping for. But it was over. There was talk of Jesus coming back to life. But Marcus had no time for that. He found that Jesus' closest followers were not causing trouble. They had stayed in Jerusalem for a time and then went back to Galilee since most of them were Galileans in the first place.

And then there was Marcus's family. Antonia and the children were not as happy as they had been. They missed their friends and the food and sights and sounds of home. So, as we would say, Marcus was stressed as he returned from the garrison one evening. Hector, his slave, had worked so hard during the past year that Marcus gave him three weeks off to travel with his friends to see some of the countryside and ancient places that interested him.

Antonia spoke, "Hector is back."

"Good, we've missed him. Lots to do," said Marcus. "Is he preparing something for us to eat."

"Yes," she said, then added, "He is different."

"Different? What do you mean?" Marcus asked.

"He has been initiated into something with the Jesus man."

"Jesus is dead," said Marcus, now slightly irritated.

"I know. I know. But... maybe you should talk to him."

Marcus sighed, "Send him to me."

In a few minutes, Hector arrived at the patio where Marcus was waiting.

"It is good to have you back, Hector. How was your trip?"

"Well," Hector began slowly, "I didn't travel as much as I had planned. My life has changed. I am a believer in Christ the Lord; I am a follower of the Way."

Marcus was guarded, interested, and suspicious. "Who is this Christ?"

"It is the Jesus who healed me, the one you and I went and listened to."

"Jesus is dead." Marcus spoke with a tone of authority and finality.

"He has risen from the dead. His Spirit lives with us. I believe and have been baptized into faith and love." Hector spoke with conviction.

Marcus was annoyed, even a little angry. "You are my slave and servant. You will not go off and join some group, just because of this new initiation."

"Master," Hector spoke with respect and love, "I will not leave you and the family. I will work as hard as ever. I care for you and Antonia and the children more than ever."

"Then what does it all mean?" Marcus asked.

"It means I belong to God in Christ. I will go and pray early some mornings. I will not go to prostitutes anymore. I will be kind and honest in all my dealings. I may not be able to carry your armor and gear into battle anymore. I cannot eat meat offered to idols; I cannot worship the Roman gods. And I will pray often."

"Well," Marcus relaxed some, "You seem to know what you will and will not do. Tell me how it all happened."

Hector too relaxed a bit. "Several of the other slaves and I went to Jerusalem. There we heard about all that had happened. We spoke with some of his closest followers. Of course, I had strong feelings about it all because he had cured me and brought me back almost from the dead. Then we heard Peter speak. He was the one chosen by Jesus to be the leader. And now he is the leader. He explained everything. I believe, and I was baptized. You should join us, Master."

"Join you?" Marcus spoke with surprise. "I am on the way to become a Roman citizen. Am I to go off and pray and eat with a bunch of slaves?"

"Yes," Hector spoke without hesitation, "Yes, that is it. Don't you remember how he told us all about the kingdom. We are all in God's love. I will continue to be your slave, but I am free in God's kingdom. You are my master. But if you don't accept God's love and forgiveness in Christ Jesus, you will still be a slave."

Marcus surprised himself by not being angry with all this. He would have to think about it.

> *Now when they heard this, they were cut to the heart and said to Peter and to the other apostles. "Brothers, what should we do?" Peter said to them, "Repent, and be baptized every one of you in the name of Jesus Christ so that your sins may be forgiven; and you will receive the gift of the Holy Spirit. For the promise is for you, for your children, and for all who are far away, everyone whom the Lord our God calls to*

him." ... So those who welcomed his message were baptized, and that day about three thousand persons were added. They devoted themselves to the apostles' teaching and fellowship, to the breaking of bread and the prayers. ACTS 2:37–42

REFLECTION

Those reflecting on the gospels often comment that Jesus saw in Peter a person of absolute loyalty, ready to do whatever was needed for his Lord. And so it turned out to be. Commentators tend to discount Peter's faults as being connected with his generosity and enthusiasm. This is likely true, but I think we can look at the relationship a bit differently.

I think Jesus saw in Peter a man much like himself. They both had strong emotions. They are the only men that the gospels report as weeping. Jesus twice wept—once over the city of Jerusalem, thinking of all the sadness it had endured and was still to face, and once after the death of his friend, Lazarus. Peter, of course, "wept bitterly" after denying Jesus.

Jesus and Peter both showed strong anger. Peter carried a sword and used it to cut off the ear of the high priest's servant. Jesus acted violently, knocking over the tables of the money changers and driving out the animals from the temple. The gospels do not record Jesus striking people with the improvised whip he used on the animals. But still his action showed very strong anger.

Both Jesus and Peter were steadfast in their mission, particularly toward the end. Jesus knew that he must go to Jerusalem to meet his fate. This was the earthly center of his world and, in its way, the founding location for his new kingdom. Jesus went to Jerusalem for the last time, knowing his fate.

Peter, like Jesus, was firmly rooted in Israel, God's people. Jesus had come for them, and to be the final Word of God for them. After the death and resurrection of his master, Peter preached boldly and bravely. Perhaps it was Peter's own preaching and how it reached people that finally made him most like Jesus. Some of the outsiders, Romans, and others accepted the message, repented, and were baptized. Peter came so see that the message of salvation must go far beyond the boundaries of Israel.

Like Jesus, who turned his face toward Jerusalem, Peter, with Paul's help, saw a new world, and the center was Rome. And so he had to be there, to preach the word of his Lord at the center of this earthly empire, to make known that the new kingdom was spreading beyond city of Jerusalem to become a kingdom for all peoples. He went to Rome knowing his likely fate. They were a lot alike: Jesus and Peter.

In the second letter ascribed to Peter, we read a beautiful passage in which he recalls his Lord.

> And I will see to it that after my departure you may be able at any time to recall these things. For we did not follow cleverly devised myths when we made known to you the power and coming of our Lord Jesus Christ, but we were eyewitnesses of his majesty. For when he received honor and glory from God the Father and the voice was borne to him by the Majestic Glory, "This is my beloved Son, with whom I am well pleased," we heard this voice borne from heaven, for we were with him on the holy mountain.
>
> **2 PETER 1:15–18**

PRAYER

Lord Jesus, we thank you for your apostle Peter. He shows us that you choose us, welcome us, and love us with all our faults. You have chosen each of us to follow you in some special way. Help us to be steadfast in our commitment to you.

QUESTIONS FOR DISCUSSION

1. Do you feel called upon to repent?
2. What is repentance?
3. What did Peter repent?
4. How were Jesus and Peter alike?
5. How were they different?
6. What changed Peter more than anything?
7. How did Peter die?
8. What does the Holy Spirit do for us?

12

Peter and Paul

CUSTOMS AND MORAL CODE

THE FIRST AND GREATEST CONTROVERSY FACED BY THE EARLY CHURCH WAS ABOUT THE RELATIONSHIP OF THE BELIEVERS IN CHRIST, FOLLOWERS OF THE WAY, TO JUDAISM. Peter and some of the others believed, for a time, that the non-Jews who joined them would have to accept the important practices of Judaism—notably, circumcision for men and the dietary laws for all. The controversy is mentioned several times—in the Acts of the Apostles and in the letter of Paul to the Galatians.

The following conversation illustrates the issues and Peter's change of heart.

"I think it is important that we talk, Peter. Just the two of us."

"I agree, Paul."

"Spreading the good news is all we both live for."

"It is, Paul."

"And yet, sometimes, I think perhaps you and the others may think I'm not quite—well, you know—one of the founders, as much a leader as you are."

"Paul, we have only one leader, one founder, and that is the Lord, Christ. The rest of us are his followers, servants, and messengers. And you have a special way—with words, with understanding. I have heard you speak, and I have read some of your letters to the communities. Your love for the Lord, your ability to tell people what they must do, and what they can become in the Lord are unequalled."

"Thank you, Peter. But we should talk about the matter of non-Jews seeking to follow the Way. How are they to be treated? What must they become in order to live the new life? I think we have some differences."

"Well? Shouldn't they read and love and learn from our sacred writings?"

Paul responded earnestly, "Of course, they should. These writings are the word of God. They tell us of the great plan from creation and through Abraham, Moses, the prophets. They help us understand Jesus, his message, and what we ourselves can become. . . . But circumcision is another matter. It is a sacred sign that we have been selected by God. But for Romans or Greeks to follow Jesus, it is not necessary. They have their own heritage and it can be grafted on to the tree of life—which is Christ the Lord. Don't you agree?"

Peter did not hesitate, "I do agree. They can join the Way of the Lord without circumcision."

Paul responded, "Good, then we are left only with the question of food."

"Yes, the food question."

"Peter, can't you see that the food is not important. Let them eat what they eat, as long as it is not offerings to idols. But other food is simply food. Didn't the Lord teach that it is not what goes into the mouth that defiles a person? Didn't he teach us over and over again that it is the Spirit that matters? It is love for one another, care for the sick, the hungry, the love of God. Didn't he tell us to live properly; to avoid adultery, anger, murder; to care for one another?" Paul went on speaking with great conviction and determination about faith and freedom in Christ the Lord.

Peter answered, "Paul, I agree. The food doesn't matter."

"You agree? The last time we spoke you were against it. You wouldn't eat with the Greeks. I convinced you? I don't believe it."

Peter spoke, "Well, actually, it wasn't you, Paul. It was a dream or a vision, or an angel. I saw all sorts of animals and a voice told me they were all from the one good God. There was no harm. Our brothers and sisters could eat and still be our brothers and sisters in the Lord. It all became clear."

Paul had to ask, "Then why did you want to discuss the food once more, just now?"

"You speak beautifully, Paul. I wanted to hear you talk about it once more. You talk about how we are one in the Lord in ways that help me understand things that were never so clear even when he was with us."

They clasped hands; they hugged.

"Peter..."

"Yes, Paul."

"Never mind."

> *About noon the next day, as they were on their journey and were approaching the city, Peter went up on the roof to pray. He became hungry and wanted something to eat; and while it was being prepared, he fell into a trance. He saw the heavens open and something like a large sheet coming down, being lowered to the ground by its four corners. In it were all kinds of four-footed creatures and reptiles and birds of the air. Then he heard a voice saying, "Get up, Peter, kill and eat." But Peter said, "By no means, Lord; for I have never eaten anything that is profane or unclean." The voice said to him again, a second time, "What God has made clean, you must not call profane." This happened three times, and the thing was suddenly taken up to heaven.* **ACTS 10:9–16**

REFLECTION

The decision about whether non-Jewish Christians should follow the rules and restrictions of the Mosaic Law was the first great controversy in the early church. It has been said that the decision in this matter determined that the followers of Christ in community were not to be a limited offshoot of Judaism but a new way of believing and living, calling to all peoples everywhere.

Down through the centuries, Christians have thought about and argued about the essentials. We, as members of that tradition and even as individuals, have struggled with matters of faith: the Trinity, Jesus as divine, how to conduct our worship. We have considered what customs of peoples far from Europe might be incorporated into Christianity because they recognize God working in this world. As a Christian people, we have tried to work out the connections between knowledge gained through study of the world around us and our faith—what we believe as Christians.

All of these issues demand and will continue to demand our attention. But unless we live as Christians, entering completely into the love that Christ left with us, we will fail in our quest for understanding and truth. And again, we can find help in the thinking of the early Christians.

Although not bound by the Jewish dietary restrictions, the earliest followers of Christ felt committed to a demanding ethical code, and they believed that their example, living that moral, Christ-like life, would demonstrate their faith. Consider, for example, the words of St. Clement about the year 150:

> So then, brothers, let us confess him with our actions by loving one another, by not committing adultery, not speaking evil of each other, and not being envious, and by being self-controlled, compassionate, and kind! We ought to suffer together the things which are hard to bear. It is

> our obligation not to love money. We want to confess him with such actions and not do the opposite.

And so it is still true that we confess Jesus as Lord and Savior in our prayers and worship, in our love, and, most important, in our lives. Paul says it best.

> So in Christ Jesus you are all children of God through faith, for all of you who were baptized into Christ have clothed yourselves with Christ. There is neither Jew nor Gentile, neither slave nor free, nor is there male and female, for you are all one in Christ Jesus. **GALATIANS 3:26–28**

Paul had come the final conclusion: as followers of Christ, through and in Christ we have entered a new dimension; we are together in God's new world.

PRAYER

Lord Jesus Christ, we thank you for the example and teachings of the apostles Peter and Paul. We ask you to help us to give our lives to you, completely. Help us to overcome the attractions of money, wealth, and lording it over one another. Help us to see all people as our brothers and sisters. Amen.

QUESTIONS FOR DISCUSSION

1. What was the first great controversy about in the early church?
2. What did Jews bring to Christianity?
3. What changed in their thinking when they became Christians?
4. What changed in their ways of acting and in their prayer?
5. What did those of Greek or Roman background bring to the church?
6. How did they change?
7. What was the great agreement about what non-Jews did not have to do when becoming Christians?
8. How does this controversy relate to issues in our day?

13

Paul and Friend

THE BODY

THESSALONICA WAS A PORT CITY IN NORTHERN GREECE, PART OF THE PROVINCE OF MACEDONIA. This city was the home of one of the earliest Christian communities and one to which two letters were written by the Apostle Paul. The first of these letters is considered to be the earliest document of our New Testament.

It would be wrong to call Eudoximes, our imagined friend of Paul, a servant of the apostle. There was nothing Eudoximes liked more than to assist Paul in any way he could, and Paul was most grateful for the assistance. They were, of course, friends, but, more important, they were bound together in a belief that had changed their lives—faith in the Lord Jesus, who had changed everything and had continued his life in them.

Eudoximes was tall and strong. He could walk all day and at a pace that would keep most men running. This was helpful to Paul, who did his best to keep in contact with the new communities of believers that were forming across the Roman Empire.

Paul was on one of his journeys and was now preaching and teaching in Corinth. He was spending a few hours working at the trade he found so satisfying, tent making. The work gave him a sense of pride and also eased his mind; he could think in his own way about the message he felt privileged to carry with him.

Eudoximes approached almost running and seemed distressed. Timothy, Paul's strong right arm, was with him. Paul looked up at them and greeted them with a quiet smile.

"The Lord be with you, my friends."

"And with you, brother," they both answered.

"You look worried. What brings you?" Paul asked.

Timothy began, "The people of Thessalonica are strong in faith and their love of the Lord is great. They remember you with fondness."

"That is all good," said Paul. "I return their love and trust. So why the concerned look on your faces?"

Eudoximes took up the conversation, "Some have died in the past few months. My own father was among them. You promised that the Day would come soon and that we would all be joined to the Lord Christ. We are waiting; we believe you. Now what will happen to my father, to the others who have died, and the others who may die soon?"

Paul was grieved. He did believe in the Day, and that it would come soon. Wasn't that part of their faith?

"Let me work for a little while and think," he said; then he went to the tent cloth and began to sew.

As he worked, Paul thought and prayed. He believed that the Lord Jesus would indeed come again, and soon. He believed he would live to see the Day. Had he misled the people of Thessalonica? He thought longer and harder. Moses, Abraham, David, all the prophets had died. Would they not be united with the Lord? Jesus himself had died; he returned to life. He was first. They would all be united with the Lord. Death was nothing to fear.

"Eudoximes," he called. "Get the materials for a letter. We must write to the people of Thessalonica." In few moments, Eudoximes was ready. Paul began to speak and Eudoximes began to write.

> *But we do not want you to be uninformed, brothers and sisters, about those who have died, so that you may not grieve as others do who have no hope. For since we believe that Jesus died and rose again, even so, through Jesus, God will bring with him those who have died. For this we declare to you by the word of the Lord, that we who are alive, who are left until the coming of the Lord, will by no means precede those who have died.* **1 THESSALONIANS 4:13–15**

REFLECTION

The First Letter to the Thessalonians, from which the verses above are taken, is judged to be the earliest of New Testament writings. Those early Christians in the small port city of Thessaloniki had taken the Good News to heart. They felt a sense of urgency based on Paul's teaching and on the preaching of Jesus himself. The end time was near. It seems that Paul and his followers would have to rearrange their thinking. Those who died would, like Jesus, be raised up and brought to new life.

And what does the risen body mean? For centuries Christians believed that this very body with which we now live would be brought together for eternal life and that life would indeed be something like a never-ending extension of this life. More recently, theologians have had different thoughts. Karl Rahner says he does not know what the risen body will be. He asks whether the risen body will have a head and says he does not know. So, what is it that we believe? To what do we look forward with faith? How are we different from those who do not have this faith?

Again, we can learn from the early Christian writings. Those who persecuted Christians sometimes took the teachings literally and tried to make sure, for example, that the bodies could not rise from the dead. An early Christian letter, written about the year 177, describes the situation:

> The bodies of those that had perished in prison, they threw to the dogs, watching carefully night and day that none of us could be buried. The remains of those who had been torn to pieces by the wild beasts and those charred by the fire they put on public view just as they were.... For six days the bodies of the martyrs, mocked in every possible way, were exposed to the elements. Finally they were burned to ashes by these lawless men and swept into the Rhone, which flows nearby. Not a trace of them was to remain on earth. This they did thinking that they could defeat God and deprive them of their restoration. They said that they should not be allowed to have any hope of resurrection, for it was through their faith in this that they introduced a strange and new religion. (Letter from Vienne and Lyons to Phrygia)

PRAYER

God Our Father, we believe as Jesus did and as he taught us to believe that death in this life is not the end. And yet, like the man who said to Jesus, "I do believe, Lord, help my unbelief," our faith is mixed with uncertainty. You ask much of us. Help us to believe strongly. We will live again with you.

QUESTIONS FOR DISCUSSION

1. What was the problem the Thessalonians faced?
2. What was Paul's response?
3. How did the early Christians have to change their thinking about the future?
4. How has thinking about the risen body changed over the centuries?
5. In what ways was Jesus' risen body mysterious?
6. Why did those persecuting the early Christians go to such extremes in destroying the bodies of the dead?
7. What do you think about the risen body?
8. On what is our hope of the resurrection based?

PART II

Images and Parables for Our Time

The second part of this book explores images and comparisons about Christian living based on our knowledge of the world around us. As mentioned in the opening pages, we do not expect to create parables or images that are better than the ones Jesus left us. But as Christians we are compelled to continue seeking the meaning of his life and teachings in our midst and for our time. Each generation must reawaken the great insights and understandings of faith.

We saw that Jesus used examples from carpentry to tell us that the care required to construct a house that will last through stormy times is an example of the care required to construct a moral life that will be faithful when storms arise. Jesus compared his connections to us to a vine and branches. And he told the story of the good Samaritan to get us thinking about who our neighbor is.

The idea and experience of weightlessness was, I think, unknown in Jesus' time. We do know what it is, although very few of us have experienced it. So it seems fair to compare weightlessness to faith. Faith should free us from the worries of this world—at least for moments. Evolution is another process, a bedrock concept of modern science, but unknown in Jesus' time. And so it seems natural to use evolution as a way of thinking about the people of God in history.

So although the framework and development of the second half of the book is quite different from the first, in both parts we are using our imagination and knowledge of the world around us to explore the mysteries that Christ, Our Lord, has left with us.

14

Light from Light

The word "light" describes a source and a power of illumination. The two go together but in many ways are separate. Consider the stars. They are points of light, offering us virtually no illumination. On a moonless night, without other light, we would be hard put to find our way by starlight. But the stars as points of light and constellations are magical and have inspired stories and legends among peoples everywhere.

We might also consider the light coming from a lighthouse. Once again, the illumination that the light throws on neighboring water or land is of little consequence. What is important—or was before the days of sonar and radar—is the message that that light gives to those on the sea about the presence of land, possible danger, and possibly a safe haven. In a similar way the pinpoint of light that trapped miners see at the end of a tunnel may offer a message of hope, though it provides no illumination. Faith sometimes seems to be no more than a pinpoint of light in a very dark cave, but that tiny pinpoint makes all the difference, giving us direction and hope.

The absence of light is often associated with danger. To be lost or unsure of oneself on a country road or a city street after dark can be worrisome. We become afraid, perhaps because of the weather or because we may become victims of violence. But more than anything, it is the uncertainty that worries us.

Darkness is often used to describe ignorance or a lack of understanding. "I was in the dark" means that I did not know what the situation was about.

A deed done in darkness means an action causing shame, one that is to be hidden, kept from the light.

When we say "Light from Light" in the creed we are referring to a light source and a power of illumination. God the Father is like the sun—an overpowering mystery that we cannot look upon directly. Yet his power is present, renewed each day in our lives.

The illumination, also Light, is the Son brought to us in the life, teachings, death, and resurrection of Jesus Christ. Through him we are able to glimpse the spiritual world around us. We can understand and gain the courage to do the paradoxical things that he did—loving those who hate us, depriving ourselves in order to help others, and believing that our suffering has value.

The sun, of course, gives warmth as well as light. We know well from the seasons of the year, the growth of plants, the renewal of energy, and other ways that the warmth from the sun is of great importance. Light without warmth can be "cold comfort," an expression used for something or someone that is intended to give comfort but really does not.

So it is with certain teachings. They may be true and even important, but they don't reach us or touch us, or for some reason we are not open and available. Consider that first Pentecost. The followers of Jesus listened and learned. They witnessed the best and the worst. We might assume that they were attached to Jesus and wanted to act with and for him. And yet, and yet—they did not or could not do anything; they were paralyzed. Then the Holy Spirit came upon them and everything changed. The light and the warmth together made the difference.

And so it has been with many down through the ages, perhaps at times for you and me. We have the understanding. But there are times of darkness, times when Light is withdrawn from us. We can feel lost and fearful, wondering why what seemed so clear should now be taken away. At these times even greater faith is needed, and faith is a gift, and so we ask that our faith be made stronger. The dawn will come, the Father and Son—Light from Light—and Spirit giving warmth will not remain distant from us.

PRAYER

Loving God, we believe that you are three in one. We do not understand, but we are happy to know you. Help us to more than know you. You come into our lives in different ways. And even deep within your being, there is community, love, and sharing. Give us, we beg, the peace and the shared love that is in you.

QUESTIONS FOR DISCUSSION

1. From what phenomenon does the creedal phrase "Light from Light" come?
2. What are some of the things that darkness symbolizes?
3. What aspects of the sun might refer to the Holy Spirit in considering the Trinity?
4. How has Jesus brought God into this world?
5. What new understandings has Jesus brought into your life?
6. How do you think enlightenment differs from faith?
7. How does the Trinity enter into your prayer life?

15

Weightlessness and Faith

We have all seen pictures of the astronauts floating in their capsules, or even outside them. They are beyond the bonds of gravity. They do slow-motion somersaults and guide themselves through space as if swimming. They are wonderfully relaxed. It is not an act of the will that provides this freedom, but it has taken enormous power for their spacecraft to escape the earth's gravitation.

Faith, complete trust in God, can make us feel weightless. It takes a lot of spiritual power to break the bonds that hold us down, and this power comes from God. With faith, we can move beyond the gravity of daily cares—work, money, and a thousand little worries. To succeed at one's chosen profession, career, or craft demands skill, dedication, and hours of concentrated effort. All of these things require an investment of psychic and emotional energy. The same can be said of relationships—within the family and beyond. Happy, successful, positive relationships require a commitment of energy, a level of selflessness. All of these activities, worthwhile and even essential, tie us down—like the ropes that tether a giant zeppelin.

But we have to see our concerns in perspective. From the air, your house, city, or town, even your country, even our planet, seems small. We are not insignificant, but we are part of something much larger. By floating for a time in God's love we can experience providence not as a fortress or wall but as freedom. We do not have to worry about proving ourselves or about what we shall eat or wear; the eternal God is holding us, letting us float.

To use a different but similar image: we know that those who dive below a rough and stormy sea find peace. Down deep all is quiet; there are fish and coral, a quiet beauty all around. But returning to the surface, life can be stormy, uncertain, even treacherous.

Jesus lived a life of faith with apparent ease. And when he spoke of faith it was often to elicit a response from someone nearby. He worked to have those around him, anyone who approached him, try to live in faith. He searched for ways to express his feelings about faith. If your faith were the size of this tiny seed, you could tell this mountain to throw itself into the sea, and it would obey you. This remarkable mixing of images reveals something of the inner life of Jesus. Faith for him was a dynamic force—a connection to God, the mystery that is beyond us and yet within us. He wanted his followers, including us, to experience that same connection. If your faith were the size of a drop of water, it would satisfy your thirst for a whole day.

Paul also experienced the connection to God that comes through faith. But unlike Jesus he did not grow up with the faith he later found. And so he sometimes contrasted faith with the burdens he once carried. He felt liberated from the weights of his previous life and wanted to liberate others. Paul argued that the works of the law—the rules for what to eat, for times of prayer, for what to do and not do on the Sabbath—were burdens. They did not liberate; rather, they kept one in doubt about whether all the duties were performed in the prescribed manner, whether one was okay with God. Even the commandments, though important for living an honest and faithful life, did not liberate Paul. He needed and found the promise of God's free and total availability to be the only answer. It was like sunlight to one who had been in a mineshaft—dazzling, almost blinding at first. But then it made everything clear.

Do we earn the gift of faith? No, but we have to let go of the burdens that have held us down. We must let ourselves be free, to experience the love and care that God is offering. Our lives will suddenly become weightless—at least for a time. Tomorrow we will have to awaken our faith once again.

PRAYER

Lord Jesus, we do believe; help our unbelief. Free us, we beg, from the worries that tie us down. Help us to see beyond the everyday work and family activities. These are important but we do not want them to keep us from you. Help us to be free, in your love.

QUESTIONS FOR DISCUSSION

1. Why do some modern, well-educated people reject faith?
2. What are some of the meanings of faith?
3. What did Jesus mean when he told people that their faith had cured them?
4. From what did Paul feel that faith had freed him?
5. How do we cooperate with God in accepting faith?
6. How do good works relate to faith?
7. What can we do to strengthen our faith?

16

States of Matter and the Trinity

As Christians we believe in a Triune God, One in Three. We believe in one God, but also that there are relationships within the very nature of the Divine. It is impossible for us to conceive of this absolute oneness, Being itself, but still with some inner life in which the divinity engages in understanding and love. And yet this thought is also comforting as we consider a God who is essentially not alone.

We cannot understand the inner life of God, but we can consider a God who relates to us in different ways. The material world is itself multifaceted. Water can become ice, which is the same and yet different. It can also become vapor, a gas that is the same and yet different from the other two states of matter.

When water freezes into ice it expands slightly; its volume becomes a little more compared to its weight. This is why ice floats and why lakes freeze with a sheet of ice on top. The ice may become very thick and strong, covering the surface, while permitting the fish and other wildlife to survive beneath. If things were just a little bit different, lakes might freeze solidly—with disastrous consequences for the living things in the water—and for us who would be deprived of so many nutrients. So ice, which is cold and hard, is important to life. In very cold climates people once built their homes of ice, walked for miles on ice, and survived in large part by fishing through the ice.

Ice is like the God who supports us, protects us, holds us up—with strength. God is indeed a loving Father.

Water, we know well, is essential for life. All animal life seems to have originated from the sea. Our bodies are themselves largely made of water. Nothing seems more delightful than a drink of cold water when we are thirsty. Water in Scripture and in our sacramental life is symbolic of life, death, and rebirth. The images of water in our lives are endless. It comes as gentle rain, violent storms, a mountain stream, a flood, and the seemingly endless expanse of the sea with its beauty, reassurance, and mystery. Water is like God, who gives life, restores and refreshes us, and even saves us. Christ, Our Lord, like water, gives life and nourishes.

And then there is water vapor, the seemingly harmless evaporation of water over time or the rapid changes as water boils into steam. Water vapor is central to the great cycle—as water becomes lighter, it flies up to the sky and prepares to nourish us again as rain or snow. Water vapor is like the hidden God who comes to us quietly, teaching and guiding—the Spirit whispering to our spirit.

PRAYER

Eternal, loving, nourishing God, you sometimes seem distant, but you are indeed as close as the air we breathe. Be with us; nourish and protect us. Guide us and increase our faith in you. Help us, as your children, to care for one another.

QUESTIONS FOR DISCUSSION

1. In what ways might God as creator and parent be compared with ice?
2. In what ways might God as teacher and savior be compared with water?
3. In what ways might God as spirit be compared with water vapor?
4. How has God entered into your life?
5. Why is it important to think of God as person or personal?
6. What image of God is most helpful to you?
7. What does it mean to say that God is both near to us and far from us?

17

Nourishing the Soul

We live in a world that has learned a great deal about the best ways to nourish the body. We know that fresh fruits and vegetables are good in many ways, that meat and fish provide protein, and that unprocessed grain foods are better than processed. We know that moderation is always good. We know that at times of illness or weakness, we have different nutritional needs.

How food turns into blood and muscle and fat and bone is quite remarkable. The acids and enzymes in the stomach and the other internal organs go to work. They sort things out, taking apart and putting together. The result is that we grow and restore our bodies and throw out what is harmful or not needed. There is not a one-to-one correspondence between what we eat and what we become. But if we eat what is good for us, the process works.

What about the life of the soul? The spirit has its needs. In Scripture, we read about God's never-ending pursuit of us as individuals and as a people. But as with food for the body, we have to digest what we read. Quoting verses to solve problems or to answer questions doesn't work. We have to take in the meaning for us as individuals, and for us as a people, in our place and time. Just as an apple in itself might be good food but only gives us strength after our body remakes it into cells of its own, in a similar way Jesus' instruction to "Go and do likewise," after the parable of the Good Samaritan, needs to be taken and transformed by each of us. Who is *my* neighbor? What must I do?

And so we need meditation and prayer to digest what we read in Scripture or hear in a homily. This does not mean hard thinking and problem solving or analysis. We simply let our minds rest. "The Word was made flesh and dwelt among us." The image and expression of the infinite came among us in love and in wisdom. And is still with us. Our minds and hearts can rest in this for a long time.

We can also be nourished by the spiritual writers of our time. Michael Casey, a Cistercian monk, shows us in his book *Fully Human, Fully Divine* how St. Mark's gospel can enrich our understanding of Jesus and of our own response to God's call. He points out that Jesus being fully human does not mean he was superhuman. We do not know what Jesus looked like. It is not likely, necessary, or important that he be tall and handsome, with remarkably keen eyesight and flowing hair. Jesus was human; he had to learn, to sort things out, to consider the best ways to teach.

The corollary of our acceptance of Jesus as fully human is that we accept ourselves as fully human. Accepting our humanity ironically is of great benefit to the soul. We should worry less about making ourselves look good, smell good, and wear all the right clothes. Some people will pay a great deal for an article of clothing, not because of what it is worth but because of who else wears it. Accepting ourselves means we accept our humanity with our failings. God in Jesus accepts humanity as it is. He expects us to do no less. Being unwilling to accept ourselves reflects an unwillingness to accept Jesus as fully human.

Jesus was himself a master of the unexpected, the mysterious, even the half understood. We are still trying to understand what he meant by the kingdom, by the Spirit he would send, and what kind of community he wants us to be. We sometimes hope that rules and plans and penalties will make us more secure. Indeed, they might, but finding God is not a matter of security. We must continually come to the task of becoming Christians as beginners. What does God have in store for us today? What surprise will I find within myself as I search for God?

In reading Scripture and those who write about Christian life, we must let the message sink in and let ourselves be nourished and strengthened. Fortunately, there is a wealth of reading and listening waiting for us. And with an open mind and heart, each reading will lead us further. As the body needs its food, so does the spirit. We don't forget to feed the body because the reminders are physically present. The spirit also reminds us every day of its needs. But the spirit whispers. The spiritual hunger pains are real, but they can be ignored.

PRAYER

God, you are a compassionate mother. A mother nourishes her child when hungry, when learning, when growing. Be with us and nourish our spirits as a mother does. Explain to us the wonderful words of Scripture. Teach us to pray—with trust and love.

QUESTIONS FOR DISCUSSION

1. Do you feel you spend enough time and effort nourishing the spirit within you?
2. What sayings or parables remind us of our spiritual needs?
3. What is prayer?
4. What is the purpose of prayer?
5. In your prayer life do you focus more on Jesus as human or divine?
6. How does reading Scripture help nourish the soul?
7. Why is it difficult to nourish your soul?

18

Evolution and the Saints

THE THEORY OF EVOLUTION DEMONSTRATES THAT GENETIC CHANGES, MUTATIONS, SOMETIMES PROVIDE THE INDIVIDUAL WITH AN ADVANTAGE, such as the shape of a bird's beak making it more suitable for a particular kind of food, or the development of lungs for breathing, or a stronger spine and legs for walking upright and moving more quickly. These and thousands of other physical advantages have occurred, and since they were genetically incorporated into the individual's body they are transmitted to his or her offspring, building a more robust species.

The theories and explanations of evolution are complex. Alongside the theory of gradual change that we hear most frequently, there is a theory called punctuated equilibrium. There seems to be a good deal of evidence in the fossil record that species do not necessarily make gradual changes over millions of years. Rather, there are long periods of equilibrium during which changes are minor. Then in a very short time, in the evolutionary calendar, dramatic changes take place. Adaptations seem to take a fast track as new opportunities are seized. In the blink of an eye, species move from water to land, or from land to air.

And we should not forget that there are evolutionary dead ends: an ecological niche disappears, and an advantage is lost.

Can we compare the progress of Christianity with evolutionary strategies?

In the history of Christianity, there are the saints and mystics and visionaries, teachers and models of what it means to follow

Jesus Christ more closely, people who are totally committed to the needs of others. These people arise in unpredictable and unexpected ways. Neither their parents nor their culture or ethnic roots can account for the way they choose to live. In fact, they are generally at odds with those around them. But they have a peculiar spiritual advantage. They see the gospel in ways that are both new and old and in ways particularly suited to their times. They take Jesus literally and apply his teachings in ways that startle their contemporaries. Mutations take place.

Perhaps the punctuated equilibrium model helps explain the new directions in Christianity. For long periods, the Church in the lives of Christians seems to go unchanged, to be in balance. Then there is a flourish of activity; new ways of living the faith are suddenly proposed and practiced.

Clearly, the mutations are not passed down physically. But after the initial shock, the saints find followers. St. Francis of Assisi lived the most radical of lives—radical in the sense of getting back to the root. He simply wanted to follow the teachings of Jesus in the clearest way, simplest way—possessing nothing, preaching the gospel as if for the first time, praying, helping those around him to live lives closer to God.

This he did, without embarrassment or apology, in a church in which leadership had become wealthy, proud, and perhaps lazy. What advantage did Francis offer in his time? It was the advantage of simplicity. He refrained from ordination to the priesthood but earnestly believed in the importance and power of the sacraments. He lived in harmony with nature but in ways that most people of his time and since have judged "too much." Even his own followers found his style of living too rigorous, his rules for living too simple—little more than phrases from the gospels. But he remains a high point in the history of the evolution of the Christian spirit. As Christians we inherit his approach; we cannot avoid or ignore who he was. He is in our spiritual genes.

St. Thomas Aquinas taught and demonstrated, contrary to many of the beliefs of his time, that faith and reason can work in harmony; reason can throw light on the mysteries of faith. Truth, wherever it is found, is of the Spirit and comes from God. Thomas felt that Aristotle, the great philosopher, should not be a hindrance to Christianity but rather should be a guide in exploring what we believe. We have been given minds with which to think. It cannot be wrong to explore the world around us, human interactions, even the revealed truths of faith.

But Thomas Aquinas should not be considered an endpoint in reasoning about the truths of faith. Theologians over the centuries have admired his spirit and his willingness to seek for a harmony between what we believe as Christians and what each generation of scientists tells us. It is important to follow St. Thomas's spirit of exploration, not necessarily all of his answers.

Dorothy Day was a different kind of spiritual leader. She lived a life of dedication to social justice—not just in writing about how to build a more just society but by serving meals to the hungry and providing places to sleep for the homeless, every day. She was a pacifist during the "good war."

There is little in the early life of Dorothy Day to account for her emergence as a model and powerful force for the poor and for justice. She grew up in a typical American family. She was in San Francisco at the time of a moderate earthquake; this was memorable but does not seem to have shaken her into a new life. As a young woman she became disaffected with the religion of her childhood, associated with political radicals, and saw socialism as a hope for society. She had an abortion and later bore a girl baby. She lived with but never married the father of her daughter.

Then something happened, a mutation of the spirit perhaps. She was drawn to Catholicism and became devoted to the sacraments, to prayer, and to reading the great works of the spiritual life. She developed a consuming zeal for the needy. Her commitment kept growing stronger—to justice and to those suffering from what she saw as an unjust society. The Catholic Worker movement has become a force in our world. The website explains that "Today over 186 Catholic Worker communities remain committed to nonviolence, voluntary poverty, prayer, and hospitality for the homeless, exiled, hungry, and forsaken. Catholic Workers continue to protest injustice, war, racism, and violence of all forms." Dorothy Day responded to the needs of her time, her world. There was a mutation, a change, a conversion of spirit, and we are all the better for it. The needs of the poor and hungry and homeless were answered in new ways.

Finally, we have the example of Pope St. John XXIII. When he was inspired to call an ecumenical council, some of those around him tried to delay. And when he would not delay, they tried to prevent the discussion from entering into new or controversial areas. But Pope John insisted there was nothing to fear, that it was time to "open the windows." And so the bishops and their theological advisors really did renew the Church. We are still digesting the ideas and practices that were introduced in areas of the liturgy, Scripture, religious liberty, ecumenism, and our understanding of the Church itself. The Church was ready, but it took the spiritual mutation from one man to inaugurate the changes.

How do we account for the spirit of total dedication and altruism found in the best exemplars of Christianity? The saints and heroes of faith changed the way we live as Christians. So it is that the emergence of saints, people of faith, like genetic mutations, is quite unexplainable. But in their lives, teaching, and example, they change things. We notice, we listen, and we try to be like them or to incorporate their ways into our lives. They contribute to the evolution of Christian faith and life.

PRAYER

Come, Holy Spirit, enter our minds and hearts. Help us to accept and better understand and live the gospel of Christ, Our Lord. Enlighten and warm us to live as Christians in our day with all the confusion and uncertainty that are part of life but also with the confidence and energy that have enlivened Christians from the beginning.

QUESTIONS FOR DISCUSSION

1. Why has the theory of evolution caused controversy for Christians?
2. What is attractive about evolution?
3. What is the evolution theory of punctuated equilibrium?
4. How are the saints like moments of evolutionary change?
5. Why does St. Francis of Assisi seem important to us?
6. What other saints or religious teachers are attractive to you and why?
7. What sorts of evolutionary change do you think the church still needs?

19

Scientific Knowledge and Christian Doctrine

TENSIONS BETWEEN FAITH AND REASON HAVE A LONG HISTORY, AND THEY CONTINUE IN OUR OWN DAY. There is a band of militant atheists, some of them scientists, who are striving mightily to discredit belief in God. They insist that the "God hypothesis" is not necessary to explain anything. Religions in general, and Christianity in particular, they say, have done more harm than good—bringing about violence of all kinds, keeping people in subjection, and holding back the progress of knowledge.

On the other hand, there is Alfred North Whitehead, mathematician, philosopher, and outstanding scholar of the history of ideas and of Western culture. He maintained that the physical sciences arose and flourished in the West for two theological reasons. The first is the belief in a God of reason, one who created a universe with order that can be understood. The second idea derives from the incarnation, the participation of God in this world through Jesus Christ. This conviction had the corollary that matter is essentially good and consequently worthy of study and exploration.

In my work evaluating educational programs I spoke frequently with students and scientists. Whether or not they believed in God, these practicing or in-training scientists shared, without exception, an absolute confidence that what they are studying can be understood. There are answers. Problems have solutions. All of nature, every aspect, they believed, can be understood. The fact that we as humans can understand the world around us, that the world has a rational foundation, is not in itself a proof of God's existence. If it were, everyone would have to believe in God. But recognizing the deep, rational foundation of things should at least make us wonder and consider that the universe has meaning. Finding that meaning is where natural science leaves off and the contemplation of mystery begins.

The progress and development of new scientific knowledge is very well documented. There are a few reliable tests, starting with: Does this theory answer questions? Does the theory explain new data better than previous theories? Is the theory predictive? Can we devise experiments or observations to test the theory?

Thinking that the earth is flat explains a certain amount of immediate data. If we walk a few miles or take measurements of a field, we do not have to take into account the curvature of the earth. But as soon as we consider more data, such as the shadow of the earth on the moon during an eclipse, or the ways in which ships appear and disappear over the horizon, or the fact that one can sail east and end up arriving back from the west—all of these and other evidence force us to shift to a spherical theory of the earth, and, of course, now we have the evidence of photographs from space.

Scientific theories are predictive in a variety of ways. Understanding the laws of planetary motion has made possible predictions about eclipses for many years into the future. Similarly, the theories of genetics enable a host of predictions about the characteristics of offspring.

The history of science is one of never-ending revision: as each theory is found inadequate to explain new information, new explanations reveal a breadth and depth that had not been previously available. And yet we find ourselves able to think within both the older and newer frameworks. We talk about the sun rising and setting, although we know that it is the earth's rotation that accounts for day and night. Newtonian physics works very well for most of our measurements of local motion, although ideas of relativity are needed for accurate GPS measurements.

What has this to do with the development of Christian doctrine? First, we are human and our understanding is always partial, always filtered through and limited by our surroundings, always in need of revision as we confront new information. Second, we learn, test, and transmit knowledge as a community.

As Christians we believe that Jesus was and is fully human and fully divine. For a long time, the prevailing understanding of how Jesus must have looked at the world derived from a "top down" approach. If Jesus was truly divine, attached to God, then he must have complete knowledge of the world, of the people around him, of the future. The problem with this approach is that it conflicts with what it means to be fully human. If we take a "humanity first" approach, we find a Jesus who faces the unknown, who has to make tough decisions, who proceeds with partial knowledge—because this is what it means to be human. Considering Jesus as fully human makes his teachings and actions even more powerful and attractive. We must never forget, however, that he is truly divine.

Are there ways in which Christian doctrine can be tested the way scientific knowledge is tested? There are, but they are not the same tests.

Perhaps the most important contribution of Christianity to the modern world is our belief that the God we believe in is a God of all people, all cultures, all languages. We as Christians have been slow to grasp and live this truth. Jesus teaches it over and over, but we want the God of all to be *our* god. We want this god to go to war with us, to protect our nation, our families.

What is the test that makes us choose the universal God over the local god? The universality of God's love has grown in the hearts of people everywhere—even those who do not believe in God tend to believe in a pervasive mystery that compels us to have compassion for others, all others. And so the corollary, namely, that we should not only feel but also do for those in need, everywhere, is widely believed.

And so every Christian doctrine should be reexamined in the light of God's universal love and goodness. If teachings and practices lead us to a deeper understanding of this love and to live it more fully, then those teachings and practices are moving in the right direction.

PRAYER

God, Our Father, you are the wisdom beneath all knowledge. You are beyond and yet within this world. When we as a people learn more about the world, we are learning more about the wonders of you. Help us to care for this world you have entrusted to us. Help us to care for one another.

QUESTIONS FOR DISCUSSION

1. What Christian beliefs support the study of natural science?
2. What are some of the things that all scientists believe?
3. What are some of the benefits of science?
4. What are some of the shortcomings in the way science is used?
5. How does a new scientific theory replace an older one?
6. What have been some of the conflicts between science and Christian faith?
7. Why are truths of faith sometimes revisited and interpreted in new ways?

20

The Seasons and the Spiritual Life

THOSE OF US LIVING IN THE TEMPERATE CLIMATES, AS THEY ARE CALLED, TAKE PLEASURE AND SATISFACTION IN THE SEASONS OF THE YEAR. Change within a predictable and stable system meets our need for growth and security. During the coldest days of January, we know with absolute certainty that spring will come. During the longest days of June, we know that darkness at five in the evening will return. We learn both urgency and resignation.

Each season has its role to play in the development of the natural world, in the growth of flowers, fruits, and vegetables. In spring, each week or two seems to have its own special blossom—crocus, daffodil, forsythia, lilac, tulip, and on they come in order, each with its own beauty and aroma. At this time, too, the sap flows, maple syrup is made, the leaves appear, and the landscape turns wonderfully green.

Summer is a time of maturation, sometimes hidden beneath the soil, sometimes very evident as tomatoes change from green to red, ripening before our eyes. The heat of summer seems to give us strength in the morning and take it away in the afternoon.

Fall is a "season of mists and mellow fruitfulness," of lush beauty and harvest. It is a time of abundance and deep satisfaction. As the days shorten and evenings become chilly, we feel that we will have to retreat from the exuberance of the outdoors to the fireside. Finally, winter is a time when all the earth must rest and renew itself.

There are also seasons in the spiritual life. They are not as well marked and defined as the seasons of the year, but they are there, nonetheless. There is a time, like spring, when we must work the soil of our minds and hearts—rooting out those habits and attitudes of judgment and unkindness that can poison and kill the good things we hope will grow within us.

There is a time, like summer, when we should nourish ourselves with the reading of Scripture and spiritual books. These will feed the inner growth that takes place quietly and slowly, deep within us, like the root vegetables that are slowly nourished, deep down.

In the fall of the spiritual life we harvest, bringing forth good things—visiting those who need help, writing to maintain the bonds of love, giving gifts perhaps of our own creation. We should let others know we are with them, together in the great mystery of color and kindness.

Then there is the winter, the time when we must retreat to prayer, to the denial of self, to find our peace and satisfaction next to the hearth—God is waiting to be with us in the quiet of the evening.

PRAYER

Come, Holy Spirit! You are the Spirit of sun and of rain, of heat and of cold, of growth and of rest. Guide us, nourish us through all the seasons in our lives of prayer, of work, and of care for others.

QUESTIONS FOR DISCUSSION

1. Why are urgency and resignation both needed by the Christian?
2. How do we tend the soil of our spiritual lives?
3. What Christian acts are like the chores of harvest in the fall?
4. How did Jesus compare growth in the natural world to the spiritual life?
5. What happens in the winter of our spiritual lives?
6. How does the image of a cycle in our spiritual lives help you pursue the goals of living as a Christian?
7. Which spiritual season do you like best and why?

21

Presence

Spiritual writers and directors suggest that we begin a time of prayer by placing ourselves in the presence of God. We might say that we are always in the presence of God, but we live with a multitude of commitments and distractions, rarely thinking about God or God's place in our lives. So we begin prayer by considering that God in fact knows us, cares for us, created us, loves us, and is present to us and within us.

But what does it mean to be in someone's presence or to say that someone is present to us? It means a number of things. If you are at home working, reading, or relaxing, it makes a difference whether you are alone or if someone else is at home with you. Even though you and your spouse, child, parent, sibling, or friend are not in the same room doing something together, still the presence of the other person is in the back of your mind. If the other person is someone you love, the presence provides a quiet satisfaction and joy. If it is a child at home after a long absence, you may feel a particular kind of happiness and connectedness. If it is someone with whom you have strained relations, then there will be disquiet inside you. In any case, something is different than when you are alone; life is shared. There are things you are likely to do or not do when the other person is present, even though not seen. You might call out to share a momentary thought or to suggest a course of action. You might simply think quietly of pleasant moments together.

Something similar happens with the presence of God in our lives. Though not seen, if we live a life that is shared with the creative power that is before and within us, then we are likely to be quietly satisfied with each hour and each day. To one who lives in the presence of God, the care and love that come from God mean that all things really do work toward what is best for us. Suffering will come, death will come, but they only bring us closer to that mystery in whose presence we now live.

There are other ways of thinking about presence. We all know well that as long as our parents are alive, we live in their presence. I recall a quick call from my daughter when she was senior in college, as excited as a small child because the first snow of the season was falling. That was it. But she knew I would like to hear about it, and indeed I did. My wife used to call her mother every evening at eight o'clock, or if she did not, her mother would call us by eight-thirty. There usually was not much to discuss, but there was a presence.

I often think of my own parents, now gone. Sometimes I recall pleasant moments—meals, days at the beach, singing around the piano. At other times I regret not having written or called more frequently, not having offered my presence or enjoyed their presence. Now they are gone, but there is still a presence. They are part of my life, and in a way, perhaps, I am still part of their lives. We are meant to share life; it is empty unless shared.

All of these kinds of human presence give us clues about how to be present to God. God is that mystery deep down within each of us and yet far beyond any of us. Knowing and feeling that God is in our lives, and knowing we can call on God, will change how we act and respond to people and situations. It is not that God is a big brother keeping track of our mistakes; rather, God is the life within us. And that life makes us not want to harm one another; it makes us want to help and care for one another. This presence is necessary for prayer.

PRAYER

God, you are within us—individually and in community. You give us life. Jesus came fully human and fully divine to share our life. We feel your presence with each breath, each conversation, each meal. Help us, guide us, and be with us.

QUESTIONS FOR DISCUSSION

1. What recent experiences of presence made you happy?
2. What experiences of presence have been strained?
3. How does technology help or hinder our sense of being present to one another?
4. What kinds of presence with family or friends has been important to you?
5. In what ways do you feel the presence of those who have gone before us?
6. What helps you gain a better sense of God's presence?
7. What can you do to increase God's presence in your life?

22

Men and Women

Not long ago my wife and I visited with friends. As we talked one evening, our friend said he had been asking people how to account for women's views of things, and what was important to them. This was not said at all in the patronizing style of, "What do women *want*?" It was rather in the spirit of admiration at who women are and how they live. Some, he said, had pointed to hormones, genes, and DNA; others spoke about the role that nature and culture have given to women. Soon the topic of conversation moved on.

There is no doubt that women and men are different. It seems to me that women typically (not stereotypically, I hope) pursue relationships while men tend to pursue achievement. There are, of course, many exceptions. Many women in business, entertainment, sports, and the arts strive for achievement. And there are men who are more interested in relationships. But more often than not, I think the type holds up. Women seek relationships; men seek achievement.

It's natural. A woman is made for others. She has room, inner space, into which she may invite a man and in which new life may grow until it is ready for the world. Even if a woman never has children, she is made this way. She nurtures, provides for others. Girls, young women, and mature women like to talk, to know each other's needs, concerns, desires, and secrets. They want to share, to help each other. We are meant to live for one another—not just as women and men, in pairs, but as people. We need each other and are much happier in community than alone.

Men want to achieve. This goes way back. Shelter, food, and protection—it was man's work to take care of these things. He had to go out, to confront, to acquire, to bring home the necessities of life. It is still so. The problem is that achievement often becomes an end in itself—not a work in the service to family and community but an effort to be viewed as strong, smart, in charge.

Can the two—relationships and achievement—join forces, work together in balance? They must. We need love, family, connections, and community. We also have a deep-down desire to explore, to understand, to achieve, and to be noticed. That's the rub, to be noticed and seen as important; then the troubles begin.

What does Jesus have to teach us? We know next to nothing about what is rightly called his hidden life—those years before he began his ministry. But based on his teachings and interactions with people, we can surmise that he was a conscientious carpenter, achieving what a good carpenter is meant to achieve—construction of a house that stands, a table that does its job, artifacts that are honest and reliable. It is hard to imagine him wanting fame or fortune for his work or for himself.

Then he entered public life and became "the man for others." His life was devoted to exploring, expanding, and deepening relationships. He responded with love and compassion to those who came near. He wanted those who would listen to accept the mystery of God into their lives in new ways. This is a God who will nurture and strengthen you. Jesus condemned relationships of power in which a person or group lords it over others. These were not relationships but situations with power at stake. "I am in charge. I make the rules. You will show your deference by following the rules."

We know the results. Jesus was humiliated and killed for who he was and what he taught. In his resurrection came the possibility of a new relationship with God for all of us. Some—through the centuries—have pointed to Jesus' victory as an achievement. He reconciled us to God, and because of that, some thought, we are better than others, able to pass judgment, to condemn, and to make rules. While there is no doubt that unity and some form of orthodoxy are important, we should never forget that it is in relationship—with God, with that mystery deep within us, and with one another—that we become what we are meant to be.

The answer perhaps, that which combines relationships and achievement, is community—for us, it is the kingdom of God. We are connected because we live in and with and for one another.

PRAYER

God, beyond us and also within us. You want us to be like you. You created with wisdom and love, and we are in awe at the wonders of creation. Help us to create good things in our own small worlds. In your inner being there are relationships. Help us to love and care for one another. Amen.

QUESTIONS FOR DISCUSSION

1. How do women and men complement each other?
2. What have been the more traditional strengths and roles for women?
3. What have been the more traditional strengths and roles for men?
4. How did Jesus change traditions in his life and teaching?
5. How does the Christian community provide opportunities for relationships and for achievement?
6. How did Jesus Christ show us the importance of relationships and achievement?
7. How does God enter into human relationships?

23

The Monarch Butterflies and the People of Faith

In the fall of each year millions of monarch butterflies end their southerly migration in the mountainous country of northeastern Mexico. The local people greet them as messengers from their ancestors. The butterflies cling to the trees in great clusters all winter in a semi-dormant state, protecting one another from the elements and resting from their long journey.

In the spring the butterflies feel a surge of warmth and energy. They rouse themselves—by the tens, hundreds, and thousands—and take to the air. They fly with absolute confidence, darkening the sky like a great northbound cloud. In Texas the butterflies pair off; selecting partners, they mate and deposit what in a short time will become caterpillars. Each caterpillar grows out of its skin three times and then dissolves into a chrysalis in which a totally new being is formed and then emerges—a newly created monarch butterfly.

The millions of newborn butterflies then fly north from Texas and into the central United States. There, this next generation matures and mates, once again creating caterpillars; and within a few weeks new butterflies emerge and almost immediately begin to fly north, continuing the journey. Further north, the process is repeated, and the fourth generation begins its life in Canada.

Then the most improbable journey begins. In the early fall, the monarch butterflies from eastern Canada begin a southerly journey, fluttering across the Great Lakes and all the way across the United States, a trip of more than two thousand miles that will take the better part of two months. This fourth generation has a greater responsibility than the others. How they manage this trip, what inner navigation and determination impels them, is a mystery. They do it and it works. Many fail and die along the way, but enough succeed in making the trip, arriving in Mexico to begin again.

We are, as a people of faith, something like the monarch butterflies. We congregate, receiving warmth and support from one another. But we are also compelled to move on. We explore both the world around us and the faith within us: we learn, we create new life, we have families, and we die. And our offspring move on, not necessarily physically. But they also explore, they create, and they carry the faith with them. As humans and as Christians we journey—encountering new ideas through science, the arts, philosophy, and our lived experience. Some generations have a greater responsibility than others because of new challenges and new ways of understanding and living out the faith. For them the journey can be longer and more difficult.

At certain times, we as individuals and as a people return to our roots—to Scripture, to the faith that nurtures us. We turn also to one another for warmth and comfort. We hold fast to the essentials; we are restored and protected. We rest, but there will always be another journey.

PRAYER

Lord God, we thank you. Through Christ, Our Lord, your Son, we have become a people. We are a people, a community, on the move. We encounter challenges, obstacles, and opportunities. Help us to recognize that what we do in this life is taking us toward you. Help us to guide and strengthen one another.

QUESTIONS FOR DISCUSSION

1. What are some of the journeys that the people of faith have made?
2. As Christians, what helps us navigate the secular world?
3. How do we pass on our faith to those who come after us?
4. What are some examples of the people of faith making progress without apparent leaders?
5. What does it mean to journey back to our roots?
6. How have the people of faith adapted to new situations?
7. What challenges might await the people of faith?

24

The Love of God

It is important to understand what God is not. I don't think it is helpful to call God the Supreme Being. Supreme Being implies that God is a being. This would mean that there are many beings—stars and animals and people and you and I and on and on. And then there is God: the one being greater than all the rest. This reasoning doesn't work precisely because it brings God down to our level, another being.

God is the source of being; God is Being itself. God is the meaning and truth that is within but beyond everything. As we grow and learn, we enter into and share in the mind and the life that is God. When we create through our work or through our families we share in God's creativity.

We share with God; we work together with all of creation and with God. We see this everywhere around us. The sun works with the rain and the earth. Elephant families work together. Bees work with one another and with the flowers. So the great plan is that all of creation should work together. But we humans are different: we can choose to work together, or we can each choose to go our own way. We can seek self, and that is when things go wrong.

But let us consider how we do, in fact, perhaps unconsciously, work together. Consider where you live, your clothing, what you eat. We benefit directly from the thousands of years in which those who came before us have experimented, learned, and passed on what is successful—in building homes, in preparing and cooking food, in making and wearing clothes. We are bound together and should be grateful in so many ways to those who came before us.

But, and the authors of the Adam and Eve story knew this so well, something went wrong. All of us in small ways or large have chosen at times to go it alone, to choose ourselves or our little group over "all of us." And that has put us at a distance from one another and from nature itself.

And then Jesus came. He taught and he lived as part of this world, as part of God. It is in caring for the poor, offering a cup of water, recognizing and doing something about the needy who are not of our group, perhaps even absorbing the violence around us—these are the things that put us in touch with God, who cares for all.

And so I think the kingdom of God might be also called the Presence of God or the Love of God. The kingdom is where God is. To better understand this, we need to do more than quote a few verses; we need to go back and immerse ourselves in the gospels. We must also remember that the kingdom of God is among us. God is Being—the root, the cause, the mind and spirit within all beings. And so it is that God is love, and love holds everything together.

But if God is love, can we love God? Is God personal? It seems more that God is power and grace and spirit but not something or someone we can love. And yet we do love God. Believers through the ages have understood that God wants our love and returns our love. How can this be?

We must look to Jesus. He found God and related to God as Father. And so it must be for us. God must be personal in our lives—whether as father, mother, friend, or, simply, the loving one. God is within us and beyond us—as the one we love and as the source of love that we give and find in others.

PRAYER

God, you are far beyond and yet within—within each of us, and within all of us together. Help us to love beyond our families, our group. Help us to give and care for those who are perhaps not like us but are part of you—God within us and among us. Help us to better love and care for one another.

QUESTIONS FOR DISCUSSION

1. How do you describe God?
2. How do you think about God?
3. How have humans worked together, without thinking about it?
4. What are some of the meanings of original sin?
5. What are some meanings of the kingdom of God?
6. What does the kingdom of God mean to you?
7. How does Jesus help us respond to God's love?
8. How can we grow in our love of God?